THE DIVERSITY ADVANTAGE

Fixing Gender Inequality
In the Workplace

Front cover design: Michelle Fairbanks/Fresh Design
Art direction: Stephanie S. Stum Photography

This book is dedicated to my mother, Seema Tulshyan.

You said no star was out of reach.

TABLE OF CONTENTS

FOREWORD

By Melanne Verveer, Former U.S. Ambassador for Global Women's Issues

Mounting evidence today—from the World Bank to the World Economic Forum—shows that women are one of the most powerful demographic groups that the world has ever seen to grow economies and advance social progress.

McKinsey and Company published the Global Parity Report in 2015, which concludes that closing the gender gap could drive between $12 and $28 trillion in GDP growth by 2025. Women comprise the fast-growing entrepreneurial opportunity to create jobs and fuel economic prosperity.

It is time to maximize the value that one-half of the population can contribute to growing economies. It's not just the right thing to do. After all, women have a right to fully participate in the economies of their countries. It is also the smart thing to do. Women constitute an under-utilized economic opportunity of unprecedented proportion.

In the United States alone, if women entrepreneurs were a country, its GDP would rank fifth in the world—close to that of economic powerhouse Germany. Women are also driving growth for companies. A study by Catalyst found that Fortune 500 companies that consistently had three or more female directors on their boards had a higher return on equity than companies with no women on their boards. Women also wield enormous purchasing power; controlling some $20 trillion in annual consumer spending globally. Muhtar Kent, the CEO of The Coca-Cola Co., put it well when he summed up the gender parity dividend: "Women are the most dynamic and fastest-growing economic force in the world today."

Yet, significant obstacles remain to unleashing the vital force that women's economic participation represents for enhancing productivity and fast forwarding us to a better world. In this excellent book, Ruchika Tulshyan lays out the case for the diversity advantage. She also does something more. She provides us with a blueprint for fixing gender equality in the workplace.

The world over, women confront a range of barriers. Women entrepreneurs face numerous obstacles—from access to credit to access to markets. A 2016 World Bank study shows that over 150 countries still have at least one law that is discriminatory towards women and keeps them from achieving their full economic potential. There are design flaws in the workplace that make it difficult to address family responsibilities and that force talented women to drop out of the workforce. Equal pay for equal work is still not a reality.

In order to realize the diversity advantage, and fix the workplace, we have to get serious about the relationship between strong economies and advancing women's careers. This book lays out the challenges from the lack of paid maternity and paternity leave to the implicit biases women face in the workplace.

Ruchika also provides the reader with best practices and solutions to address the inequality issues that are holding back progress. From male champions to flexibility in the workplace, and from examples of companies which are leading the way, this book provides a toolbox filled with tools to fix gender inequality in the workplace.

We learn not just *why* this is a win-win for companies, economies, governments as well as women and their families, but also *how* to bring about the changes that are required to realize the diversity advantage, across the board.

INTRODUCTION

"Companies must change if they are going to attract, retain and best leverage their female talent. ... We can no longer afford to allow talented women to be educated and trained, but not have an opportunity to succeed and thrive."

—Becky Blalock, author of *Dare: Straight Talk on Confidence, Courage, and Career for Women in Charge*, and former chief information officer of Southern Company

When Sukhinder Singh Cassidy, founder and chairman of the video shopping platform Joyus, moved to Silicon Valley nearly two decades ago, after a successful career in media and investment banking, she was excited to begin a new career in technology.

Shortly into her first job in the tech sector, she was told by her managers that she "scared the secretaries," without any explanation. She wondered: Was it the way she spoke, the way she walked or her natural intensity? Things went downhill from there. She was originally hired to negotiate strategic partnerships at the company, but instead she was given the job of rewriting marketing collateral. "After being given increasingly junior tasks and watching a volatile male colleague's behavior get rewarded, I considered leaving the Valley altogether," she wrote in an article for Re/code.

About 10,000 miles away in Singapore and close to two decades later, another woman ponders the future of her career. Sharon, whose name has been changed to protect her identity, is three months pregnant and has just been offered a new job as an account director at one of the largest digital agencies worldwide. But she's conflicted: Should she let her new employer know about her pregnancy before she signs

4

the contract? Will she risk being considered less competent and committed in the new position? She worries the offer may be rescinded or renegotiated. Her husband, who works at another multinational corporation, faces no such dilemma.

These two very different women, in different parts of the world, represent some of the major obstacles that working women tackle regularly. Women face the risk of being relegated to junior tasks or being phased out of key projects because their commitment is questioned when they become mothers. Employee engagement in the U.S. is alarmingly low at 30% today, costing organizations up to $550 billion in lost productivity, finds **Gallup research**.

By not addressing these issues, companies are losing talented, ambitious women in high numbers. It's bad for women but equally bad for businesses and the world economy.

Women: The Next Billion

Close to a billion women will enter the global workforce by 2020, especially from India and China. But without making fundamental changes to organizations today, these women are likely to drop out or get stuck in dead-end jobs. That's a tremendous economic opportunity, if leveraged correctly. Gender inequality is rampant in the workplace today, even among the world's most developed economies.

As the world contends with slowing economic growth driven by constraints on labor market supply, engaging women could be a key driver of global economic growth, economist Nouriel Roubini tells me. "In places like Japan and South Korea, some of the most highly educated women drop out of the workforce, while many markets are facing labor market shortages due to aging populations.

Companies must provide the economic opportunities for women as a matter of priority."

Organizations of the future, whether they are made up of two employees or 200,000, must step up to help talented women be successful. Simply hiring more women doesn't solve the challenges of retaining women or creating an organizational culture where women thrive and advance. Over 50% of university graduates are female in developed economies, but the number of women in senior leadership and/or board positions within the Global 2000 is alarmingly low.

The U.S. is the only developed country that doesn't guarantee paid maternity leave to female employees. Women are largely paid 77 cents to a white man's dollar for equal work—and this number decreases significantly for women of color. As a journalist, I've interviewed countless successful women who had to network in male-dominated cultures and usually stuck out like a sore thumb. And even then, they were rarely invited to take the very top jobs.

Too much of the existing narrative focuses on "fixing women"—getting more women to negotiate, assert, demand, be confident and "lean in" to leadership. Research backs up the existing confidence gap between men and women. But confident women have also confessed that it's not enough for women to simply "lean in," to borrow a phrase from Sheryl Sandberg's 2013 campaign. When corporate structures cannot accommodate for the fact that women may want to be mothers and caregivers while also progressing in their careers, "leaning in" falls short. In recent times, women like PepsiCo CEO Indra Nooyi and former U.S. State Department director Anne Marie Slaughter have vocalized the guilt faced by working mothers. Smart organizations must realize this and equally "lean in" to support their female employees in order to build a robust pipeline of female leaders.

Make no mistake: This is no feminist manifesto. Sure, gender equality is a human rights issue. But engaging women in the workforce is primarily an *economic* issue. Diverse leaders drive bottom-line growth and high-level innovation for global corporations.

This book isn't only for women or chief inclusion officers or HR practitioners. It offers insight and case studies on why it's a priority for *everyone* in an organization. To attract, retain and promote women, the best companies worldwide have made inclusion part of their culture, driven right from the top. Many of these strategies I outline tie in strongly with retaining and advancing millennial employees too.

Diversity isn't just the right thing to do. It's also a financially savvy strategy in today's hyper-competitive digital marketplace.

1

WHERE ARE THE WOMEN?

When your company embarks on implementing a diversity strategy, one question must be asked at the get-go: *Why?* Just as when you are expanding into a new product line, undergoing geographic expansion or even making major cutbacks, it's the "why" that justifies the change. Creating a more gender-balanced workplace is no different.

Diversity sounds great in principle—the desire for a fair and equitable workplace for all is a moral right. But this alone hasn't moved gender inclusivity far beyond a cursory afterthought in most organizations. Indeed, to drive an initiative that really works, we need to look at the impact on the bottom line.

Will having more women on your team result in greater profitability? Actually, yes. If companies want to prosper and retain their business advantage, they would benefit from having a diverse workforce, new McKinsey research finds: "Companies in the top quartile for gender diversity are 15% more likely to have financial returns above their respective national industry medians."

While correlation does not necessarily mean causation—greater diversity doesn't automatically mean more profit—the link indicates that companies committed to diverse leadership are typically more successful. Aligning the commitment to diversity with financial goals can get the skeptics to at least think about it.

Next, consider: Who are you selling to? This question is at the heart of why a diverse workforce is so necessary. Women in America have immense spending power today, ranging from between $5 trillion and $15 trillion annually. And it's growing. Approximately two-thirds of consumer wealth will be controlled by women in the next 10 years. Whatever your company is selling or servicing—whether it's soap or software—chances are women have a large, if not majority, influence over it. If your leadership team doesn't have enough female representation, consider the tremendous missed opportunity to get into the mindsets of your largest customer base.

Steve Bucherati, the former chief diversity officer of The Coca-Cola Company, told me that the founding of Coke's Global Women's Initiative was largely spurred by the fact that Coke's leadership team looked nothing like its leading consumers. Until 2007, 70% of the company's product purchasing decisions were made by women—but only 23% of the leadership was female. In just over six years, the company made incredible strides forward in diversity. Now more than 30% of Coca-Cola's senior leadership team is female. The efforts to change the ratio were driven from the top: CEO Muhtar Kent has tirelessly championed advancing women throughout the organization at all levels. The result is a sea change in the way high-potential women are hired and advanced at the company.

But making diversity a priority doesn't require you to have Coca-Cola's coffers. The first step doesn't require money—just commitment to hard truths.

First, assess your brand. "Look at how you're perceived in the marketplace," says Phil Hendrickson, a talent acquisition expert with previous experience at Starbucks, Apple and Sapient. This requires an organization to be brave, inquisitive and ready to face uncomfortable realities. "Your company's brand is your best recruiter, working 24 hours a day and driving interested job seekers to search and inquire about your jobs. It works in the reverse as well. If you have a bad reputation, then it will subvert your other outreach activities." This is your starting point, from which all other recruiting activities can be assessed.

Fixing the way your brand is perceived for female employees starts in incremental steps. Evaluate your existing hiring practices by looking at which candidates apply and get a job at the company, by gender and experience. "The first step is in collecting data on how you're hiring right now," says Joelle Emerson, founder and CEO of Paradigm, a consultancy on creating diverse workforces. Collecting gender breakdowns on who applies for jobs within your company, who is invited to phone screens and in-person interviews, and finally, who actually gets a job offer, will produce powerful data that can be harnessed to make a change. "With this data, you can be strategic and specific on what's next."

One mistake Emerson sees is often organizations leap headfirst into a diversity initiative, without recognizing the barriers within their existing hiring practices. At every step of the recruiting practice, different organizations often put up different barriers to attracting high-potential women.

It can start right from the job description. Women are less inclined to respond to listings containing words like "determined" and "assertive," as these words are connected with male stereotypes, according to research from the Technische Universität München on how leaders are selected and assessed.

The researchers showed approximately 260 test subjects fake job ads, containing frequently used words. What they found was astonishing: If the ad described numerous traits associated with men, such as "independent," "aggressive" and "analytical," women were less likely to apply. Women were more attracted to descriptions containing "dedicated," "responsible," "conscientious" and "sociable." Men, on the other hand, were not deterred either way.

In the past, one technology company, Buffer, used to advertise software developer positions as "hackers." After noticing a dismal rate of female applicants—2%—the company experimented with using "developer" instead. The company hired its first female engineer soon after making this change, and shortly after had two full-time developers who were women. Buffer spokesperson and head of content marketing Courtney Seiter adds: "We are still very new to this area and learning so much every day. Our next step will be to figure out the most responsible and ethical way to track and measure some of the demographics of our candidate pool to determine what level we're at now and how we can improve."

Textio, a program that uses big data to predict the effectiveness of a job description, finds that words like "nerf" and "rock star" in job listings attract more male applicants. The software advises companies on how to optimize job listings so the best candidates apply, regardless of gender.

It's also important to note whether your job listings explicitly state a commitment to diversity. Textio analyzed over 10,000 tech job listings nationwide and discovered that only 34% of companies include even a minimal equal opportunity statement, according to a blog post by Kieran Snyder, the company's founder. Your job listing is often the first interaction your company has with your dream candidate.

Isn't it worth figuring out how to best represent yourself?

Where Are You Sourcing Talent From?

Hiring managers at companies often complain that not enough women apply for the roles advertised. Much of the time, the advertisements are not reaching a larger cross-section of applicants.

Teams both within HR and outside need to have talent sourcing strategies to connect with different talent segments, according to Hendrickson. It's not just a matter of finding people in IT, finance or engineering, but also looking for segment-specific diversity categories—for example, "women in IT or African Americans in engineering," he says. "We would identify where to advertise our roles, where to source from, where to network for talent and what groups to become members of. There are many segment-specific groups on LinkedIn and on other social channels where recruiters can begin networking and building relationships for candidates and referrals."

Hendrickson also encourages his recruiters to attend professional women's conferences and to join groups from social networking portals like Meetup.com to extend the talent pools of female candidates. The key is to look beyond where you're currently recruiting your candidates.

Referring Diverse Applicants

Fostering a culture of inclusiveness starts at the top, says Shellye Archambeau, CEO of MetricStream. The Silicon Valley-based governance, risk and compliance firm raised $60 million from investors last fall and a total of $125 million since its inception in 1999.

Most people are likely to have individuals who look like them in their immediate networks. Archambeau says modern workplaces must encourage hiring managers and human resources support functions to start looking beyond their traditional networks when creating the talent pipeline. "Recognize and reward managers that are creating diverse teams," she adds.

It's a missed business opportunity if your team is homogenous, while your clients and consumers are of different backgrounds and genders. "Diversity really helps teams thrive. Even an all-female team of the same ethnicity is not as successful as a mixed team."

Hiring from a diverse pool of candidates is top of mind for Dan Shapiro, CEO of innovative startup Glowforge. "I feel like it's suicide to miss out on diversity. We would be foolish to miss out on representing the massive population that make up our customers," says Shapiro, whose company claims to be creating the world's first laser 3-D printer. Shapiro was previously at Google, after selling his last company to the behemoth. Realizing that only 12%

of Glowforge's applicants were women, he introduced a referral bonus in June 2015 that would give non-employees $5,000 if they referred a successful candidate who was a woman, underrepresented minority or person with a disability. "We have a particular challenge in that our founding execs are all white men. That narrows our perspectives and our recruiting networks. While we're fortunate to have a steady stream of amazing resumes from people who want to help us, far too few of them represent the full diversity of the customers we want to delight with our products," Shapiro wrote in a blog post announcing the initiative. As of September 2015, the company hired three new women, including two female engineers. "One specifically mentioned that the [referral] program was a part of why she wanted to join," Shapiro wrote to me by email. Intel also recently announced it would pay employees a referral bonus of up to $4,000 if they referred a successful female, minority or military veteran candidate. Selecting from a bigger pool of candidates will naturally increase your chances of hiring the best fit for your company.

Unconscious Biases

Another major blind spot can be whether your company judges male and female candidates equally. When managers were not given any information about the candidates other than their physical appearance, managers of both genders were two times more likely to hire men over women for a math-related task, according to a study published by the *Proceedings of the National Academy of Sciences.*

Even when the managers were shown that women completed the tasks just as well as men, the male candidates were still 1.5 times more likely to be hired than the women were. Moreover, whenever a lower-performing candidate was hired, two-thirds of the time the lower-scoring candidate was male.

"Until hiring and promotion practices change, women can 'lean in' all they like, graduate in record numbers from top universities and dominate buying decisions—but they still are much less likely to make it to the top," writes gender strategist Avivah Wittenberg-Cox in a *Harvard Business Review* article discussing the results of this study. "The corporate world is led by men confident that they are identifying talent objectively and effectively. The reality, underlined by this and many other reports, is that decision-making about talent is rife with unconscious assumptions and personal biases."

One company, GapJumpers, is seeking to correct for these unconscious biases by putting candidates through "blind auditions" for a job. In general, female applicants face three obstacles: fitting into company culture in male-dominated companies and teams; being questioned about their commitment and their skills; or being hired just to fill a quota, GapJumpers cofounders Petar Vujosevic and Kedar Iyer tell me in an email interview. By using a technique similar to the one on the hit American television show *The Voice*, job seekers apply to open positions by answering a "challenge" question on a deadline set by an employer. Employers don't see the names or credentials of the applicant—just their answers. On GapJumpers, female applicants score higher than men on rigor, attention to detail and presentation skills, the cofounders tell me. Based on data from more than 1,200 blind auditions across 13 companies, GapJumpers found that more women agree to participate in blind auditions (54% women), more get selected for interviews after these auditions (58.6% women) and a whopping 69.2% of women get hired. "Even well-meaning people sometimes skew their hiring judgments unconsciously, because of shortcuts our brains have internalized over a long period of time. Blind auditions are key to eliminating implicit hiring bias," according to the company's website.

Paradigm's Emerson works with clients on training hiring managers on their unconscious biases when they interview candidates. Part of this entails using a gender-neutral vocabulary to describe job positions. It also means creating a uniform feedback system to justify the reasons a candidate was hired or rejected.

Does Your Interview Process Repel Women?

One of the most memorable job interview processes I've personally had was at a pioneering technology company. I was interviewed by five men, over a four-and-a-half-hour period, with no breaks. These so-called "pressure tests" are famous in the tech industry.

Every 40 minutes or so, I would speak with yet another employee at the company who looked nothing like me, whom I couldn't relate to. The process made me repeatedly question whether I could realistically see myself working there and also if I would be a good cultural fit. I was offered, and ultimately ended up taking, the job. As advertised, the work was exciting and the pay was great. But indeed, my team ended up having very few women, and the work culture in my department reflected archaic gender expectations. I quit within a year.

"In traditional workplaces, interview panels are still common," says Pavita Cooper, cofounder of Elliott Cooper Partners, a London-based headhunting firm. "It's important to reflect on who you're asking the candidate to meet. Are there women? Make sure it's not just the same token woman appearing at all interviews, but interviews should represent a wider cross-section of women at your organization." Cooper, who sits on the steering committee of the 30% Club, an organization launched in the U.K. with a goal of achieving 30% women on Financial Times Stock Exchange-100 boards by the end of 2015, believes that when interview panels or loops are made up of "pale and male" interviewers, women feel disengaged during the process.

"I work with senior-level women all the time who will come to me to ask, 'Why aren't there more women at the top level at this organization? Is the culture not a good fit for women?'"

Emerson agrees. "Diversity in the interview loop is a best practice used by the most innovative organizations." Apart from including female employees during the interview process, it's also key for interviewers to ask each candidate the same set of questions. "An interview process that's optimized to be unbiased is not just to hire diverse candidates, but really to hire the best candidates," she adds.

Create A Company Narrative Around An Inclusive Culture

While asking about a woman's marital status or plan to have children is against the law—rightly so—Cooper recommends making it a best practice to discuss work culture and inclusiveness during interviews. Most high-potential female leaders look for a work culture that highlights support for employees to have a life outside of work, she says. When interviewers discuss the work culture, and even how they achieve balance within the organization, it can communicate a work culture that's infinitely more attractive to female leaders. "If a male interviewer brings up topics like family in an interview, it signals to the interviewee that she's more than a robot just being hired to do a job," she says. Of course, if your company doesn't make provisions for employees to succeed outside of the workplace, then it's not possible to sell it in the first place. But that's reserved for a later chapter.

"It's important to talk about your company's culture in a thoughtful way," adds Paradigm's Emerson. "Establish a company narrative on culture, one that every employee is able to talk about to potential hires." Training hiring managers on unconscious biases has been a strategic part of Emerson's consulting business for tech companies. "It's about making every effort to take the bias out of decisions across the board—from hiring to compensation to promotion. Recognize where your hiring managers may have biases, and work towards building a vocabulary that includes everyone."

While he was developing talent strategies for Starbucks and Apple, Hendrickson says website testimonials on the work culture from *existing* female employees were a draw for potential women candidates. "Recruiting is everyone's job, so involving the business in interviewing is vital," he says.

Human resources must equip recruiters with the skills to discuss the career trajectory of women employees at the company and how the business is supportive of professional development.

Brand Ambassadors

"Develop the women who work for you now. They are your best spokespeople," Hendrickson adds. In his experience, current female employees can often produce the best referrals and speak best to why working at the company is a great career move for other women. "Every one of your employees is a brand ambassador, so develop your female employees and enlist them in your recruiting events, your interviews and other strategies," he says.

Rethinking diversity at the recruiting level doesn't have to be an onerous or expensive process. It's important to take an honest look at your company's diversity practices right now—then develop a strategy to remedy a few processes that need immediate attention.

2

EQUAL PAY FOR EQUAL
WORK TAKES WORK

Courtney Seiter knows exactly what her boss earns. And what her boss' boss makes. In fact, she knows right down to the last dollar what every single employee at her company, Buffer, is paid. The social media company made a daring move in 2013 by publicly releasing each employee's salary, together with a comprehensive revenue calculator that shares base salary per role, with a percentage bonus for seniority, experience and location. As a content marketer, Seiter's $94,000 compensation puts her in the higher bracket of the profession, according to PayScale, a company that tracks salary data. She also knows without a shadow of a doubt that she isn't being compensated differently because of her gender or negotiation skills.

"I felt secure for the first time in my working life that I was being paid what I deserved and what I was worth," says Seiter, on working in this salary-transparent environment.

This level of openness isn't found in most organizations—in fact, pay is one of the few topics that remains taboo and even prohibited at work. But with this secrecy, we continue to operate in an environment where pay inequities are rampant and systemic. While pay secrecy in America is widely practiced, it has led to consequences such as a significant salary gap between executives and junior employees. It also perpetuates gender pay disparity. Needless to say, pay secrecy is outdated and even harmful in today's environment, where technology has driven transparency in various areas of the workforce; it's now common to share photos of your employee experience on Instagram or tweet about your colleagues. For organizations that want to stay relevant and attract the best talent, salary transparency must feature as a key strategy.

First, a quick look at the gender pay gap today: In the U.S., pundits quibble over the exact disparity between what women and men are paid for equal work. You've likely heard the numbers 77 cents, or 78 cents, or 80 cents to the man's dollar. But regardless of which angle you look at it, women are consistently paid less than white men for the same work—across industries, professions, qualifications and locations.

Around the world, the statistics are just as grim. Differences in pay and employment opportunities result in large lifetime income gaps for women, according to U.N. Women's 2015 Progress Report. Over the course of their careers, French and Swedish women will earn 31% less than men. For German women, the gap is a surprising 49% and a whopping 75% for women in Turkey.

The report also finds that women's labor force participation has stagnated over the past 25 years worldwide, led by significantly low female participation in Central and Eastern Europe and Central Asia, East Asia, the Pacific and South Asia, which account for close to 60% of the global female population of working age. Some explanations include political changes (the fall of state socialism in Central and Eastern Europe and Central Asia meant more women stayed home) and negative social attitudes towards women working in South Asia. The fact that only half of women participate in the labor force, compared with three-quarters of men, is indicative of the persisting worldwide gender gap.

One of the biggest obstacles to resolving the gender pay gap is denial. Most CEOs or senior leaders believe their companies would never discriminate by gender. No, theirs is different—men and women must be paid equally for equal work, they think. They believe that neither gender nor race plays a part in determining compensation. And yet, women are largely paid less than men regardless of qualifications and capability, across all levels of the organization and around the world. According to *Bloomberg*, even the highest-paid female executives take home an average of $5.3 million dollars—or 18% less than their male peers in the S&P 500.

"Most organizations don't purposefully create policies that are discriminatory," according to a whitepaper produced by PayScale Inc. "Usually, there has been an adverse impact on a certain protected group that was not intentional. These unplanned, negative situations can be troublesome because, although there was no intent to discriminate, the law does not require intent when it comes to discriminatory pay practices."

Indeed, today many organizations award compensation based on a vague ballpark figure of what a position should pay, at the discretion of managers and often based on how well an employee negotiates. In short, compensation is awarded based on subjective, not objective, information.

Don't Reward The Best Negotiators

Studies show women are less likely than men to negotiate salary offers and raises. Because of this, women stand to lose up to half a million dollars in compensation over the course of their careers, according to Carnegie Mellon University professor Linda Babcock.

Any forward-thinking organization today will recognize that there are social obstacles to negotiating. Expecting all employees to negotiate is rarely the most equitable way to compensate. Men tend to negotiate often and negotiate for more. Then, there are cultures such as mine—Indian and Singaporean—where asking for money is not only considered ungrateful, but highly offensive, whether you're male or female.

"When we put all the responsibility on individual women to close the pay gap by asking for more, we ignore the very real issues that employers need to address, like unconscious bias," says Lydia Frank, senior editorial director of PayScale.

"Women can pay a high professional cost just for asking, because both men and women have deeply ingrained expectations about how men and women should behave, what's appropriate. When women behave outside that social norm, they're punished for it," she adds. In essence, when women ask for a raise or negotiate a higher offer, they often don't get the higher number, or when they do, they're considered less likable. "Studies have shown again and again that we, as a society, believe that assertiveness on a man looks like confidence, while assertiveness on a woman looks like aggression," says Frank.

An article in *New York Magazine* stated: "Asking women to take responsibility for closing the pay gap with their ace negotiating skills is sort of like teaching women self-defense as a way of addressing sexual assault. It puts the burden on women to figure this out as individuals—it doesn't ask much of employers, and it doesn't really address the bigger issue."

I truly believe corporate culture is ripe for change in this regard. With all these social conditioning barriers, it's surprising that salary negotiation has continued as a practice for so long in corporate culture. Women, especially, face a double whammy when they negotiate.

There are two possible ways to fix this. Find a way to overcome social conditioning so women are not penalized for negotiating—easier said than done—or take the negotiating tactic off the table entirely. Some companies have started incorporating this practice.

In April of 2015, Reddit's then-CEO Ellen Pao told *The Wall Street Journal* that the company doesn't negotiate with candidates during the hiring process. "Men negotiate harder than women do and sometimes women get penalized when they do negotiate," she says. "So as part of our recruiting process we don't negotiate with candidates. We come up with an offer that we think is fair. If you want more equity, we'll let you swap a little bit of your cash salary for equity, but we aren't going to reward people who are better negotiators with more compensation."

Dan Shapiro, CEO of technology startup Glowforge, says salary negotiation is similarly discouraged at his company. "As a strategy, I find negotiation is gender-biased. I refuse to hire based on a candidate's negotiating skills," he tells me. Instead Shapiro evaluates median salary data for the positions he hires for, then gives candidates a "second-best offer," in which they can either ask for more equity or salary, which adds up to each person in the same role being compensated equally. "I don't want people to feel like they're missing out on salary. At the same time, I want to hire people who are more excited about the work than the compensation."

Recognizing these differences between male and female candidates, Disney ABC Television's VP of talent acquisition Daisy Auger-Dominguez has a "secret" strategy to ensure women and men are paid equally when they are hired. "I sometimes offer women a higher number because I know they're not going to negotiate," she told the audience at The Next Billion conference in May 2015. While this solution is not sustainable—or entirely fair—Auger-Dominguez says it's necessary for organizations to understand and internalize that men and women negotiate (or don't) salary differently and learn how to work around the social conditioning to ensure their employees are being paid fairly from the start.

Asking The Tough Questions From The Top

Evaluating how your employees are currently being paid is a directive that comes right from the top. Evaluating salary data shouldn't just be the job of human resources; in fact, leaders from across the organization should be involved. Forward-thinking CEOs of multi-billion-dollar companies are starting to pay attention. In April 2015, Salesforce CEO Marc Benioff told *The Huffington Post* he was reviewing the salaries of 16,000 employees to make sure that male and female workers are paid fairly.

Already Benioff says he's given some women raises. "I expect to be giving a lot more," he said in the *Huffington Post* interview. He anticipates that the process will take a couple of years.

"My job is to make sure that women are treated 100% equally at Salesforce in pay, opportunity and advancement," he said. Though he didn't know what the pay gap between men and women was at Salesforce, "when I'm done there will be no gap," he says. Initiatives like the one Benioff has undertaken are both uncomfortable and resource-intensive for the employer. Which company would want to admit it's engaging in discriminatory practices? And yet, innovative organizations that want to remain competitive cannot afford to ignore this. It is better to know where you stand and take corrective measures than to lose out on key talent, tackle distrust among employees or—worse of all—have to face an expensive lawsuit.

Consider eliminating pay secrecy in your organization. According to results from the IWPR/Rockefeller Survey of Economic Security, almost half of all workers nationwide are discouraged or even contractually forbidden from discussing pay with their colleagues. With pay secrecy in place, employees struggle to find out how their pay measures up with peers. Any attempts to fix the gender wage gap are also undermined. Where there are high levels of pay transparency, the gender pay gap is much smaller: The report finds a comparatively small 11% wage gap within the federal government.

"Greater pay transparency, along with strengthened enforcement of U.S. EEO [Equal Employment Opportunity] laws, a higher minimum wage, more collective bargaining and better family-friendly policies, such as paid family leave, would go a significant way towards ensuring that working women are paid fairly and are better able to support their families," states a recent Institute for Women's Policy Research report.

Getting The Right Data

Being equipped with unbiased salary information is key; this helps companies compare how they're paying employees with up-to-date market averages.

"Using data to set compensation is also critical for an organization, because going with your gut or surveying a handful of professional contacts can really backfire. Employee compensation is the single largest expense for most businesses, so you can't afford not to be making decisions based on the best available data," says PayScale's Frank. "When you use data to drive your compensation strategy and practices, you avoid unintended pay disparities between workers of different genders, races, etc."

It's a good idea to show employees the numbers you're looking at to help them understand how they're being paid relative to the market for their position. "Using data and being open about what data you're using also helps employees understand that you're not pulling a number out of a hat."

Transparency around compensation can result in healthier work cultures based on trust. A recent PayScale study found that of employees who felt they were underpaid, only 45% actually were. The remaining 55% were paid at or above market. "That false perception, though, can turn into discontent and you can end up losing some of your best employees simply because you're not being open and sharing information," says PayScale's Frank.

"Salary transparency can take many forms, from just being more open about how you set salary ranges to sharing everybody's exact salary," she says. "When you're transparent about your compensation practices—how you define your labor market, which data sources you use to set salary ranges, why each employee falls where they do within the given range—you're fostering better relationships with your employees."

It's equally important to keep assessing salary data with regular "check ins" on how you're paying employees for the same work. There are a plethora of tools now to find up-to-date salary information by industry, experience, location and qualifications. Once you have defined your labor markets for talent and set your ranges, it's much easier to share those ranges with employees. "Not every employee needs to see every range, but why not share their own salary range for their position with them? By opening that dialogue, you're starting down a road to transparency and really to more satisfied, engaged employees who trust the organization," Frank adds.

How Gap Inc. Pays 137,000 Employees Equally For Equal Work

In 2014, global clothing retailer Gap Inc. publicized data to show that its male and female employees were compensated equally for equal work. This claim was independently verified by Exponential Talent. After analyzing a data set of pay information for Gap's approximately 137,000 employees around the world, the consultancy found no significant gender wage difference for the same jobs at Gap, worldwide and by region.

According to Eric Severson, Gap's former senior VP of global talent solutions (who left shortly after this interview), the company made two monumental announcements in compensation that helped establish its role as a leader within the industry for women. In 2014, the company announced it would raise the minimum wage across its U.S. stores to $9, followed by $10 a year later. According to Severson, year-on-year job application numbers at Gap grew by 24%.

In the same year, Gap also published that its compensation was equal across roles, between genders. While equal pay wasn't necessarily a corporate decision at the get-go, Severson says gender equality has been a strong cultural value at Gap, as the company was cofounded by a woman, Doris Fisher. Once the company started evaluating compensation data in 2014, it realized there was no significant difference in the way men and women were paid. "We made a decision to publish the numbers, and like our minimum wage increase, saw our competitors following suit. Other companies may start investigating their compensation data too."

"Both these moves helped us in our goal of wanting to be the best place for women to work in," he says. "We believe what's good for women is good for business. When you provide pay or opportunity equality, all boats rise and everybody benefits."

According to Severson, good governance within Gap was key to achieving gender-neutral pay. According to him, there are three key reasons for Gap's pay equality achievement.

1. Equality Of Leadership Representation
"At the company, for many years, we've had more women than men in leadership," says Severson. At the store manager level, 69% are female and perform the bulk of hiring and pay decisions. Across the company, 74% of Gap employees are female. "If you want women to be represented equally, you need more women in leadership roles making hiring and pay decisions," he says.

2. Equality In Flexibility
According to Severson, women are often penalized for asking for flexibility—including a reduction in pay or

advancement opportunities. Gap adopted a Results-Only Work Environment (ROWE) where employees are evaluated on performance, not their physical presence in the workplace. While the benefits of flexibility including ROWE will be discussed in the next chapter, from a compensation standpoint, it has ensured that neither gender is penalized for working flexibly.

3. A Culture Of Equality From The Top
"Gap was founded in 1969 after the civil rights movement, so diversity was always part of our strategy," says Severson. The company's CEO Glenn Murphy has made multiple statements on how everyone in the organization must look out for equality. Governance at Gap means every pay decision is overseen by HR and measured and regulated. "You make a choice to invest in that oversight. We have instated lots of checks and balances to make sure managers can't exercise any individual bias in making decisions," he adds.

While the company hasn't "calculated the announcement of pay equity to our earnings," Severson expects it to have a positive impact over time. "Over 80% of our workforce is made up of millennials, and we know millennials as a generation have a disproportionate concern for social justice, equality." Severson also pointed to the high social media traffic to the pay equality campaign. "That tells us our customers care about this."

Lessons From The Small Gender Earnings Gap In Pharmacy

Harvard University professor Claudia Goldin has conducted some of the most comprehensive research around earnings and the gender wage gap. In her *Milken Institute Review* article, Goldin states that pharmacy is a high-income profession with a small gender pay gap and almost no penalty for clocking in few hours.

"Pharmacy underwent major changes in the last several decades. Self-ownership and the fraction working in independent practice plummeted from 1970 to the present," her report states. Female pharmacists make up about 60% of all workers in the profession.

Her research finds that most pharmacists today are employees who work for large firms and hospitals. Better technology and the standardization of drugs have allowed for pharmacists to seamlessly hand off clients and be good substitutes for each other. As a result, short and irregular hours are not penalized and pay is almost perfectly linear in hours. "Those who work fewer hours—say, because of family responsibilities—are paid proportionately less. Part-time work is common, especially for women. But there is almost no part-time wage penalty," Goldin's paper states. More organizations would benefit from noting changing expectations in the workplace: It's become more desirable for workers around the world to work flexible hours or telecommute, but few would choose flexibility if it amounted to a significantly lower wage. The next chapter focuses on why flexible and output-oriented workplaces are an important strategy for gender inclusiveness.

Before you turn the page, there's a number I'd like you to consider. The World Economic Forum predicts that we won't have global gender equality at the workplace until the year 2095. Are you willing to wait that long when some of the solutions are well within our reach?

The State Of The Gender Pay Gap In The U.S.

1. The gender wage gap for full-time/year-round female workers was 22%—or 78 cents to a man's dollar—in 2013. That year, women's median annual earnings consisted of $39,157, while men earned $50,033. If the annual earnings ratio continues to change at the same rate as it has since 1960, men and women won't reach parity until 2058, according to data by the Institute for Women's Policy Research. Over a woman's 40-year career, she will be paid nearly half a million dollars less than a man in the same period.

2. Women make less than men in virtually every profession. On a weekly basis, male surgeons make $590 more than female surgeons, and male CEOs make $455 more than female CEOs. Male-dominated professions are also consistently valued higher than female-dominated ones. For example, truck drivers (made up of 95% men) make an average weekly wage of $730, compared with $418 for child care workers, a profession in which 95% are women.

3. The gap widens significantly when evaluating pay for women of color. African American women earn 64% of what white men make, while Hispanic or Latina women make 54 cents to the white man's dollar. Asian American women are the closest to achieving parity, making 90% of white men's earnings. But this can't be bridged by education alone. In fact, the gender pay gap only increases with higher education for black, white and Hispanic women.

3

GIVE YOUR EMPLOYEES FLEXIBILITY WITHOUT SHAME

Corporations around the world are losing their best female employees largely due to one unchecked flaw— lack of flexibility. On the one hand, we have the ability to perform a multitude of tasks with just a portable laptop and steady Internet connection. "Going to work" could have been largely transformed by the type of technology that exists today. The keyword here is "*could.*" Unfortunately, even many workplaces that offer flexible work policies in theory still penalize employees who are not always in the office.

Sallie Krawcheck, former president of Global Wealth and Investment Management for Bank of America, recently addressed the flexibility problem in a fiery LinkedIn post. Companies are not slipping on diversity numbers for lack of trying, she wrote. "Working women who choose to have children are breaking into two broad groups: One works full-time, holding on, exhausted, through their children's younger years. A full 60% of these moms wish they had a flexible work option," she writes. The women in the other group—5.4 million of them—leave work during those years, only to pay a hefty economic price. "On trying to re-enter, 73% report trouble finding a job; and those who successfully do so suffer precipitous drops in income."

Companies seeking to attract the best talent will build cultures and career paths that are much more advanced than current flexibility approaches by enabling true "flexibility without shame." They will recognize the tremendous opportunity that technology brings to foster new working styles—and that being able to engage employees fully part time can be much better than engaging them distractedly full time.

Krawcheck's assertions hit the nail on the head: Whether organizations offer flexible work arrangements or not, when women ask to work flexibly, they are met with resistance, fewer advancement opportunities and an overall feeling of guilt.

How big of a problem is this for the future success of organizations? Monumental, according to three leaders who work with women in leadership positions around the world.

"The No. 1 reason the highest-potential women leave jobs is not compensation, it's invariably a lack of flexibility," Pavita Cooper, steering committee member for the 30% Club tells me.

"Women leaders, particularly of the Millennial Generation, think of companies without a flexibility value proposition as dinosaurs and often seek to work elsewhere," according to Aniela Unguresan, the cofounder of Switzerland-based EDGE Certified Foundation.

"One of the main reasons why women opt out of full-time paid work is not because of long hours, it's because they don't have control over their work schedules," says Shelley J. Correll, director of Stanford University's Clayman Institute for Gender Research.

It was interesting to note how three women leaders in three distinct parts of the world, with very different skill sets, agreed on this one thing.

Workplace flexibility is particularly important for women who often balance multiple significant roles. "Such practices influence attraction, promotion and retention—and future representation—but also drive engagement and productivity," recommends a Mercer study, "When Women Thrive, Businesses Thrive." However, enjoying flexible work options shouldn't have to come at the expense of career growth, the report states.

Somewhere along the line, the intention to foster a gender-balanced workforce fell out of line with existing office culture. This has been felt sharply in the U.S., which until recently had among the top female employment rates worldwide—a peak of 74% for women aged 25 to 54 in 1999. Today European countries have overtaken this number while U.S. female workforce participation has dropped to 69%. How do we approach turning this number around?

Workplace Flexibility Is Good For Employees And Employers

In a landmark study of over 44,000 employees in 18 territories on the work expectations of millennials—the generation born between 1980 and 1995, consulting firm Pricewaterhouse Coopers (PwC) found that 71% of its millennial employees (compared with 63% of non-millennials) reported that the high demands of work intrude on their personal lives. The firm undertook this study after finding their millennial employees were leaving the firm in record numbers compared with employees of other generations. The study wasn't broken down by gender except a section that found that 15% of male workers and 21% of female workers would accept a lower salary and a slower pace of promotion in return for fewer work hours.

Another study conducted by FlexJobs surveyed 1,500 job seekers looking for flexible work arrangements. Work-life balance featured as the No. 1 reason respondents of both genders were seeking a flexible work schedule. Over half of those surveyed also reported that when completing important assignments they preferred their home to the office.

The reason I'm highlighting gender-neutral data first is that expecting a flexible work arrangement is not a women's issue. Sure, in the way society is structured today, more women are still in charge of child-rearing or caregiving and therefore would benefit from this arrangement. But it's increasingly becoming an expectation of employees of both genders. Anecdotally, when I surveyed five different friends who manage teams at large companies like Amazon and Deloitte as well as smaller firms, they all said that they receive as many requests for flexible working arrangements from male millennial employees as they do from women. These friends were not authorized to speak to media and agreed to be interviewed on the condition of anonymity.

There's good news for the employers in there too. In fact, some research shows it can be even more beneficial for organizations than for employees when companies offer flexible work arrangements. The FlexJobs survey found that flexible work options offer companies various benefits apart from the real estate savings they would enjoy from not having to accommodate full-time remote workers. In addition, according to the survey, one-fifth of respondents would take a 10% pay cut for flexible work options and 22% would give up health benefits. A further 18% said they would be open to working more hours in exchange for flexibility. Companies could potentially benefit from higher employee retention; 82% responded that they would be more loyal to their organizations if they had flexible work options.

There are consequences if companies don't catch on: 39% have turned down a promotion or job or quit over lack of flexibility.

A Workplace Trends study also found employers, too, reap greater benefits from their flexibility programs. Work-flex programs improved employee satisfaction, say 87% of HR professional respondents, while 71% saw increased productivity and 65% reported retention of current talent. Sixty-nine percent cite the programs as a "recruiting tool" and 54% believe that the programs yield positive benefits when it comes to recruiting.

The business case for what I call an output-driven environment (versus one where long hours and in-office face time are valued more) is well established. Yet, the inertia against adopting output-driven environments—and not penalizing employees for making use of flexible work arrangements—is still a major hurdle to be overcome.

Especially when women work remotely, they are likely to be considered less productive and often do not get promoted at the same rate as employees who don't work flexibly. This often creates gender pay inequities too.

Making Flexibility A Standardized Norm

As it stands, women are severely penalized for requiring flexibility in companies that do not make flexible work arrangements part of their culture, or where flexibility depends on individually-agreed-upon scheduling that varies by manager and teams. Instead, the key is to have an environment where flexible work arrangements are considered both gender-neutral and an institutionalized part of the culture.

"We've seen that the world's biggest companies have phenomenal offerings around flexible work. But when we ask employees if they feel judged for using these policies, we often find they are operating in a face-time environment, not output-driven environment," says EDGE's Unguresan. "My advice is don't offer flex-time if you're only offering it to women. You are identifying a population of your workforce as having special needs and it will hurt their career." Instead, all leaders I spoke to for this chapter emphasized the importance of having top-down, gender-neutral commitment to flexibility, where it becomes the norm—not an exception for a select group of people.

So, what has worked at some of the world's most innovative companies?

It's important to identify if you really need these arrangements, and whether current programs are working. One of the easiest and cheapest ways to find out the state of flexible working arrangements in your organization today is by anonymously surveying existing employees.

Vodafone, the British global telecommunications company, has been a leader in this movement for a few years. In 2012 the company won a *Harvard Business Review* and McKinsey prize for its innovative approach to mobility and flexibility, in its pursuit of creating a less hierarchical and more open environment. Vodafone shares a five-step action plan for organizations on how to approach flexible work arrangements. I've adapted and edited it for length below.

1. Evaluate
Learn the unique dynamics of your organization. Seek to learn the average makeup of your employees and whether they are given the freedom to work remotely. Are workers held accountable for specific results? How does your

organization measure productivity? "Through a number of simple studies, employee and leadership interviews and observation studies, you can quickly get a clear picture of how your workplace is functioning," the report recommends.

2. Gather And Educate
Assemble a change leadership team by identifying key people. They must agree upon a common vision of "better business." Use the information you glean from the workplace studies mentioned above to make targeted goals.

3. Classify
Sort your employees into groups: fixed, fixed-mobile, mobile and home workers. The report recommends using observation, online surveys and workshops to discover how your organization currently supports these four types of employees. "This builds the business case for change by shifting the traditional fixed profile of a 'worker' to a much more flexible and mobilized workforce," the report says.

4. Plan For Change
Based on your goals, define how much change you need. See if every employee needs office space every day, or if it would be more effective to move to smaller offices. What technology do you have that would enable your employees to work flexibly? This blueprint will define how altering your space, use of technology, employee behaviors and processes will deliver better results.

5. Transition
While the short-, medium- and long-term changes may come as a bit of a shock to your employees, introducing both immediate and gradual benefits can help employees to adapt. The transition will take time and can only be successful if employees are engaged and supported through the changes.

Vodafone U.K.'s advice is actionable and the first few steps revolve around taking the pulse of your organization at where it is today, then planning for where it needs to be tomorrow. As with all initiatives described in this book, real change starts from the top and must consistently be linked with business benefits—this includes employee engagement.

According to research from Catalyst, flexible work environments do not have to be limited to knowledge workers. The research shows that even hourly-wage employees who are given flexibility can tremendously improve results for both employees and employers. In fields where telecommuting may not be an option—such as retail, warehousing, manufacturing and child care—Catalyst recommends:

"Think creatively about flexibility in your workplace. Can your organization make small scheduling changes— such as shift trading, relief pools [substitute teachers, for example], flexible start/end times to shifts, half-day vacation increments, employee-designed schedules, shifting assignments based on availability and skill rather than seniority, and unpaid time off—that could result in big workplace improvements?"

How Flexibility Helps Leaders Thrive

In 2008, Gap Inc. transformed to a formal Results-Only Work Environment (ROWE). If there were a scale to measure office working styles, ROWE would be at one extreme end, while the traditional 9-to-5—with desk cubicles and managers being able to know the whereabouts of each employee—would be at the other end.

According to ROWE, people can work from home absolutely anytime, without having to make excuses or provide an explanation. Also, there is no vacation or sick time—employees take off as much time as they see fit. In return for this freedom, workers must produce. Bigger-picture expectations are set and how those goals are met have nothing to do with how many hours are logged at the office.

Gap Inc. adopted ROWE in 2008, but had a flexible working environment for years before.

"We believe our high representation of female leaders is related to us always being able to offer flexible working arrangements," Eric Severson, Gap's then-SVP of global talent solutions, tells me. According to him, ROWE's innovative approach is "built for the 21st century" and gives employees "the freedom and accountability to meet both personal and work/customer needs by using their own ingenuity."

"ROWE has been our secret weapon, as none of our competitors have adopted it," he tells me. The initiative is gender-neutral, as the concept of asking for flexibility is eradicated—flexibility is institutionalized in the culture. So whether male or female employees work flexibly, or don't, they are valued by their productivity, not face time.

"ROWE builds trust and requires a lot of trust. ROWE is not about work-life integration; for us it's about revolutionizing the work environment from the industrial to the knowledge age. The idea that management is about watching people physically working is outmoded," adds Severson.

So how did Gap make the shift to ROWE? Severson describes a particular challenge the company was facing in a department where a new technology in e-sourcing required one San Francisco-based department to work around the clock to negotiate with Hong Kong vendors. "We saw incredible burnout, up to 40% turnover at one point, because this team would work all night in Asia time, go home for a few short hours and be back at work to work America hours," he tells me. "We knew something had to change; the employee engagement in that division was at the lowest of all our divisions at the time."

Gap piloted ROWE initially in just that department. Within six months, that division had the second-highest employee engagement and turnover was half of what it was before. Through a pilot program, Severson's team was able to test what worked for their company and what didn't. Soon after, ROWE was rolled out across the organization.

"My advice is to pilot any flexible work environment in a small part of the organization, then measure and test against the productivity in other parts of the organization," he says. "Start small, then scale."

ROWE, or a similar model, may not be for everyone or all industries. Indeed both Best Buy—where it originated from—and Yahoo announced ending ROWE practices. Still, some form of flexible work arrangements must be implemented where knowledge workers exist.

Leaders Must Visibly Use Flexibility

Output-driven environments normalize new working styles that have been enabled by technology. But current environments that have not institutionalized these working styles into the culture penalize women for working flexibly by limiting their growth opportunities within the company.

According to previously cited research by Mercer and EDGE, there is higher female representation overall in organizations where 33% of the workforce (or more) avails of flexible work benefits. Basically, when only women make use of these work arrangements, it doesn't increase female representation at the company, but when a third or more of *all* employees do, the organization retains more women.

I acknowledge that flexible working arrangements aren't an option for all companies, especially ones that are smaller or in industries requiring large numbers of hourly workers. Here, creating a culture of openness is key, says EDGE cofounder Unguresan. "Nothing works better than having senior leaders in organization, male preferably, who start working differently," she says. "For example, if a senior male leader announces he is going to start working four days a week, or stands up in an internal meeting at 5 o'clock and says he's going to pick up his kids but will be back online later." According to Unguresan, when senior leaders make it publicly known they are availing of the programs offered by their company, "this shows flexibility doesn't hinder your growth, and you're actually rewarded for making use of it."

For DeLisa Alexander, chief people officer of software multinational Red Hat, her personal experience shaped how she influenced the company to view flexibility. When she joined the company as general counsel 14 years ago, she negotiated a schedule with Fridays off to care for her child. It was unusual for the time—but Alexander knew she needed it to be successful.

"I was able to participate and shine and even pulled into a leadership development program. In due course, I progressed into a VP position even with a flexible schedule, one that was even more flexible for a time after my second child," she says. Currently, 25% of the company's 7,100 employees work remotely. "Employees who want to work flexibly are often less attractive to other companies, but I always thought we should think differently and be talent-focused here."

Alexander admits that at times it has meant higher costs to accommodate a remote workforce in the short term, but she points out the benefit of retaining talent and differentiating as an employer of choice in the long run. Time and again, leaders I've interviewed for this book have mentioned the short-term costs of implementing a dedicated flexibility program—money, time, efforts to change culture—as a tradeoff worth making for the long-term benefits of an engaged, loyal and high-performing employee base.

Manager Training Around Flexibility

Flexible working arrangements are most successful when they are approached from the top down, and both Unguresan and Alexander point to the importance of manager training around this.

Here's the reality—the working world has changed rapidly and four generations often work side by side in the same company. For many managers, working styles and norms have changed dramatically since they entered the workforce. To create a supportive flexible work environment that doesn't penalize women for making use of flexibility, managers must be equipped to work with people they may not see all the time.

"Our managers are very good at vetting flexible work requests and determining the value the associate is providing," says Alexander. "Our focus with managers is around training to develop associates to be their best. It's 1:1

management. For us, we value the personal relationship between manager and associate so the manager knows the strengths and weaknesses of their associates and also what they need to be successful at work."

Unguresan says the difference often comes down to the way managers approach flexible work arrangements. "Managers today need a different set of skills to preserve team spirit and how teams work together," she says. "It's also important for organizations to train managers around the different tools that help get the team together no matter where they are in the world."

Alexander says a successful initiative around this includes regular manager meetings and trainings around leadership development. She also points to the company's robust online community of Red Hat managers, where employees actively share best practices on what helps their teams be successful. "We're all learning how to be managers in the 21st century and how to be successful in managing a diverse workforce."

There's no question that technology is changing the way we approach work today. What is surprising is the number of offices that still operate with a model where long hours of in-office time are valued over output. As technology—and the expectations that come from working in a digital environment—continues to disrupt traditional offices, smart organizations will work towards fostering an environment where employees are trusted to deliver their best work from anywhere. Given how rapidly the workplace is changing today, an output-driven work environment is not just a valuable retention strategy for your best female employees, but a way to keep your best workers, regardless of gender.

4

REVERSING THE MOMMY TRACK

In trying to reach a global audience, this chapter will no doubt divide readers by geography. Paid maternity and paternity leaves vary significantly by country, largely due to government policy on the subject. But one underlying principle is common among the majority of working women around the world—they have the ability to bear children. While not a new phenomenon, many employers around the globe have still not found the best way to provide support for employees with children. Long working hours and expectations to be constantly connected intersect with rising costs of child care around the world. Many women—and increasingly, more men—are starting to opt out of the workforce to strike a balance. As a result, organizations are losing out on female leaders.

In the U.S., where the majority of the organizations I interviewed for this book are headquartered, paid leave statistics are abysmal. America is the only industrialized country that doesn't have a government mandate to provide workers with any paid leave. The existing Family and Medical Leave Act of 1993 gives only about half of all workers 12 weeks of unpaid leave for birth or medical conditions. In this regard, the U.S. trails far behind nations like Pakistan (12 weeks paid at 100% of salary) and Sudan (eight weeks fully paid).

Many women who can afford to leave the workplace after giving birth do, as evidenced by falling female workplace participation rates in America. Any form of parental leave in the U.S. is at the discretion of the employer.

Some corporations offer leave based on the perceived scarcity of the employee's skills. Low-income women, who often work in jobs that don't provide leave, can fall into sustained poverty after becoming mothers.

By contrast, much of Western Europe guarantees mothers paid leave for nearly a year—an average of 40.5 weeks, with Finland offering over three years of paid maternity leave per child. However, no country or corporation has perfectly figured out how to offer support for working families without losing top women. Countries that don't offer paid maternity leave, such as the U.S., are contending with thousands of trained women who leave the workforce after they give birth. These women often struggle to find opportunities when they want to return to work. Even in countries with very generous paid maternity leave—all of the Scandinavian countries, for example—there's research to show that women suffer in other ways: They lose out on pay, leadership opportunities and even access to professional networks.

This chapter outlines how the ideal scenario lies somewhere in between; policies must dictate adequate paid maternity and paternity leave and support for child care if the expectation is to have all employees working long hours. This wouldn't prove to be a great retention strategy just for women, but also for newer entrants to the workforce. A 2015 EY Global Generations study found that 38% of millennial workers—male and female—in the U.S. are so frustrated by the lack of paid parental leave policies, they would be willing to move to another country with better policies. To retain and advance the best employees, especially women, organizations must accommodate workers who are—or want to be—parents.

The Case For Adequate Paid Maternity Leave

The International Labor Organization recommends an average of 14 weeks of job-protected paid maternity leave for female employees. In the U.S., where only three states (California, New Jersey and Rhode Island) require paid leave for parents, innovative companies are taking matters into their own hands to attract and keep top female talent. Organizations like Google, EY and Bank of America pay out of pocket for paid parental leave, ranging from 10 weeks to 39 weeks of paid parental leave.

To be sure, these multi-billion-dollar corporations are not just providing this benefit for a feel-good reason. The data is undeniable—paid leave increases employee retention, which saves organizations money. Replacing workers is expensive: Turnover costs account for about 20% of an employee's annual salary, according to research from the National Partnership for Women and Families. Employees are more likely to quit when they don't have access to paid leave.

In a global study commissioned by Vodafone U.K., KPMG found that providing paid maternity leave has the potential to boost businesses worldwide by $19 billion in savings.

The KPMG study estimated that:

- It costs global businesses a whopping $47 billion annually to recruit and train new employees to replace the women who leave work after giving birth.

- In contrast, if businesses were to offer women 16 weeks of fully paid maternity leave (rather than only adhering to the legal minimum), it would cost businesses just $28 billion more.

- Businesses would save up to $19 billion a year if they could get women to return to work after taking maternity leave. Moreover, instead of having to train a new worker, they would retain the experience and knowledge of these women, leading to enhanced productivity and effectiveness.

- Working mothers could cumulatively save $14 billion if companies offered a global return-to-work policy that allows them to work just four days a week, at full pay, for the first six months after they return to work.

Acting on data from the study, Vodafone announced it would be one of the first organizations in the world to implement a mandatory minimum maternity policy. By the end of 2015, female employees in Vodafone's 30 operating companies in the United States, Europe, Africa, the Middle East and the Asia-Pacific region will be allowed at least 16 weeks of fully paid maternity leave. For their first six months after returning to work, they'll be allowed to work 30 hours a week at full pay.

Could we see more U.S. companies following suit? Again, the data would make sense. When Google increased its paid maternity leave to 18 weeks, the rate at which new mothers left the company dropped by half.

Google executive Susan Wojcicki—the CEO of YouTube—wrote an impassioned op-ed in *The Wall Street Journal*, making a case for why paid maternity leave is good for business.

"It's much better for Google's bottom line—to avoid costly turnover, and to retain the valued expertise, skills and perspective of our employees who are mothers. ... Best of all, mothers come back to the workforce with new insights. I know from experience that being a mother gave me a broader sense of purpose, more compassion and a better ability to prioritize and get things done efficiently. It also helped me understand the specific needs and concerns of mothers, who make most household spending decisions and control more than $2 trillion of purchasing power in the U.S."

Wojcicki herself is proof of a company's success when it provides great maternity leave—she was the first "Googler" to go on maternity leave and has taken it four other times since in her 16-year career there. After coming back from her second maternity leave, Wojcicki led the creation of AdSense, one of Google's most profitable businesses.

While public policy on this issue needs a dramatic overhaul in the U.S., paid maternity leave is quickly becoming a benefit that more employees expect. When I speak with millennial peers, I find that most appraise prospective employers on review sites like Glassdoor.com and search specifically for a company's maternity leave policies when deciding on whether to accept a job offer. The EY study cited earlier found that 48% of millennials would avail of paid parental leave when they had children, more than any other previous generation. Even if they aren't planning to ever have children—or any time soon—knowing that they're working for an inclusive environment that values families is important.

ThoughtWorks, a global IT company, recently increased paid maternity leave to 12 weeks and offered five weeks of paternity leave. The company also provides out-of-pocket financial support for employees exploring options such as in-vitro fertilization, adoption and surrogacy.

The decision to support working families was a deliberate retention strategy, for an industry that requires highly skilled workers and tends to have a hard time attracting women. "We felt it was very important to support all our workers and ensure we're making the most appealing proposition to work for ThoughtWorks for folks who are starting families," said Joanna Parke, North America managing director for the company. "We prioritized a variety of diversity initiatives about five years ago and we've seen a rapid rise in women that apply to and stay on at ThoughtWorks because of our concerted focus on inclusiveness."

Parke said given the difficulty in hiring and retaining specialist technical talent, offering better maternity leave than its competitors has helped ThoughtWorks retain its competitive advantage. "Women tend to leave when they're not supported by their employers. When we saw the cost of that extra benefit [of paid maternity leave] versus the cost of hiring someone new to fill the position, it was a no-brainer."

At the same time, paid maternity leave goes beyond just the policy aspect to be effective. It's essential to train managers on how to ensure female employees are not "off-ramped" during their pregnancy or when they return to work. Having set goals and targets, as well as a dedicated action plan—such as giving employees flexible work schedules—will ensure women are not penalized when they go on maternity leave. While a woman's job may be legally protected, employers must be actively involved to ensure she does not come back to reduced responsibilities or find that she's been taken off the promotion track.

Paid Maternity Leave As A Matter Of Government Policy

The lack of statewide paid maternity leave in America is largely a political issue. However, companies large and small must understand the benefits to their own bottom line if they offer paid maternity leave.

Both at a policy and at a company level, this area is ripe for disruption. States that have more comprehensive maternity leave policies—like California—will continue to have a hiring advantage. This isn't just relevant to businesses in knowledge industries or who hire specialized workers. "In California, which has had a state paid leave program for more than a decade, 83% of workers in 'lower-quality' jobs who used the program returned to their previous employer— a 10-point improvement compared to workers who did not use the program," according to research from the National Partnership for Women & Families. In every industry, employers that get ahead of the curve early are likely to keep and advance their best female employees. It is also necessary for companies to lobby for government support in assisting smaller organizations with providing paid maternity leave, just as governments all over the world do. The costs are just too high to ignore for the company and society as a whole.

Some are optimistic about how America can take the lead on this issue, perhaps even making child care subsidies part of law in time to come. "Because they are so late to the game, I think the U.S. has a unique opportunity to innovate and lead the way on policies to do with working parents," said Anna Steffeney, a former IT executive and founder of LeaveLogic, a startup that helps companies implement maternity leave benefits. Steffeney, who gave birth to one of her children in Germany and the other in the U.S., experienced firsthand the marked difference in the maternity leave policies of the two countries. In Germany, 14 weeks of paid maternity leave, along with job-protected unpaid leave (if parents want to take time off until their child is three years of age), is legally mandated. In America, no *paid* maternity leave is required by law. Federal law guarantees job protection for employees taking unpaid maternity leave, for full-time employees who have worked at the company for over 12 months and only if the employer has more than 50 employees.

Distrust Of Mothers: The Mommy Track And Parental Leave

Providing paid maternity leave is only half the battle for working mothers. The fact is that *globally* mothers are hired the least, perceived as being less competent or committed and even paid less than male counterparts with equal qualifications.

"There is a pretty strong stereotype that mothers are less committed to paid work," according to Stanford's Correll.

In 2007, Correll conducted a study in which researchers sent out fake resumes to employers. The resumes were all identical except for one difference: Some mentioned the applicant was part of a parent-teacher association, which indicated the applicant was a parent. The study found that mothers were half as likely to be called back by these hundreds of employers, while men with the parent-teacher association had a higher call-back rate than the applicants whose resumes did *not* indicate parenthood. A separate study by Correll also found that in new job offers, mothers were extended on average $11,000 less than women without children and $13,000 less than fathers. As such, fathers were the most preferred by employers, while mothers were least preferred. Mothers were also held to more stringent performance standards.

Unsurprisingly, the data disproves the employers' views that women are less productive. In a study of over 10,000 economists, researchers at the University of Zurich, the University of Konstanz and the Federal Reserve Bank of St. Louis found that raising children had no negative impact on productivity among employees. In fact, economists with children were slightly more productive than their childless peers, but it wasn't a statistically significant difference. Still, the myth that mothers are less productive persists.

This is a cultural bias that can't be addressed by better maternity leave policies. In fact, negative perception of mothers can often run rampant in countries and companies with the *most* generous leave policies, according to Switzerland-based EDGE's cofounder Aniela Unguresan. Taking maternity leave often translates to less advancement opportunities for a woman, even in situations where her job is protected, said Unguresan.

"Instead, *parental* leave is the solution that levels the playing field," she said. "Providing long maternity leaves that keep women for so long out of the workforce are a negative influence, but what's successful is providing paid maternity leave that's between six to eight months, and beyond that, parental leave where both men and women take time off from work," she said.

Currently, employees of both genders can face negative perceptions for being visibly involved parents. "In the U.S., the 'fatherhood bonus,' where fathers are perceived as more committed employees and paid better, is only relevant in cases where fathers are not visibly involved. Fathers that actually take paternity leave face the same biases as women who take maternity leave," Correll said. But the fact remains that more millennial employees are coming to expect parental leave.

"We need these leaves to be available to mothers and fathers and we need policies that apply to both men and women. We need to create culture where policies are available and not frowned upon for being used," she said.

To counter the side effect of long maternity leaves in Iceland—that women were still largely responsible for child care—the country adopted a new system offering a total leave of nine months for parents, giving mothers and fathers three months of paid leave each and three months to share. The government also mandated a use-or-lose policy; fathers couldn't defer the leave for later. As a result, 90% of fathers took paid leave in Iceland and child care was equally shared by nearly 70% of parents who lived together.

When parental leave becomes widespread, the benefits are multi-fold. First, it proves that employees of both genders can be highly productive while also being parents. Second, getting employer support to take care of children would become culturally accepted, not just another way to discriminate against women in the workplace.

The World Economic Forum's Global Gender Gap Report has consistently found a strong correlation between countries with strong economies and those that advance women's careers. For many countries, this has meant retaining highly educated, high-potential women who also happen to be mothers. Countries that provide paternity leave foster a culture where men are more present in their households, while more women stay on in the workforce. Gender equity is achieved on both the home and work fronts.

To be sure, women suffer a double whammy as mothers—they're perceived as being less effective at work, and the high cost of professional child care and unwillingness of male partners to share child care duties can sap their time and energy. As much as 60% of professional women in America who stopped working said their husband's unavailability to shoulder household and child-rearing duties led to their decision to leave paid work.

In the U.S., prohibitive maternity leave policies—or a lack of them—lead to more women opting out of full-time paid work or getting stuck in middle-manager roles. In many European countries, the glass ceiling is also fortified by maternity leave, but in those cases, it's because managers become reluctant to hire women in their child-bearing years, anticipating long absences or less commitment to work. To combat this, countries like Norway, Iceland and Germany now offer incentives to encourage men to take paternity leave.

"Again, companies have the opportunity to change social culture and stigmas," said EDGE's Unguresan. "Having generous paternity leave and creating a culture where men and women are equally encouraged to take time off from work will continue to be a differentiator for the best companies." Women will be less stigmatized for becoming mothers when parents of both genders are seen as providers and caretakers. In a world where dual-income households are becoming the norm—78% of millennials have a working spouse, compared to 47% of baby boomers, **according to** EY—it's absurd that companies continue to operate with policies that were set in place decades ago.

Lactation Rooms And Child Care

The financial cost to companies that lose qualified and trained women is high. There's an alarming imbalance if you consider that more women than men graduate from college in America, and yet 43% of women with children leave their jobs. Again, innovative companies continue to dominate the market because of the opportunities they offer to women with young children. In the U.S., it is federal law for companies with over 50 employees to allow female employees "reasonable break time" to pump breast milk in a private space that is not a bathroom. Surprisingly, this has been interpreted by many smaller businesses to mean conference rooms and other areas where women can be interrupted while pumping. Setting up private lactation rooms could be a game-changer for organizations, especially in an environment where the fastest-growing segment of workers are women with children under the age of 3.

At the same time, the high to prohibitive cost of child care has also become a reason many high-performing female employees opt out of the workforce. This is particularly the case when women are married to a high-earning spouse and it makes economic sense to drop out of full-time work.

While some companies in America have realized the benefit of subsidizing child care for their female employees, it's still a largely unusual employee benefit.

Instead, we're seeing more innovation in countries like India, a country that has one of the lowest female labor force participation rates in the world. Citibank India offers employees a child care allowance over and above their salaries to spend on day care services of their choice. (However, the same benefit is not offered to Citibank employees anywhere else in the world.)

"It is always a challenge to retain women in their mid-careers, as marriage, maternity and mobility tend to take precedence over professional growth," Anuranjita Kumar, chief HR officer of Citi, South Asia, tells me. Citi recognized that these key life events would impact the majority of its India-based female employees and created policies to help them pursue and grow their careers, she says. "We believe organizations have a significant role to play in creating leadership opportunities for women. The reality is women usually have a larger and a more sensitive role to play in motherhood when compared to their male counterparts. During this period, organizations need to step in and support this transition."

Kumar also adds that if a woman feels let down at work because of motherhood, her leadership journey is surely impacted. Indeed, businesses in India have been contending with how to engage more women in the workforce—where only 20% of Indian women are working today. Organizations that have strategized early are enjoying a competitive advantage in attracting, retaining and promoting women in India. Citi India also made other landmark changes to attract and retain more working mothers: Its flexible maternity policies give women the option to use their 180 days of leave either continuously or stagger them at the employee's convenience.

In contrast, fewer companies are spending on child care benefits than ever before in the U.S. The National Study of Employers in the U.S. found that the number of American companies that are offering payments for child care (through vouchers or other subsidies with direct costs to the company) has fallen from 5% in 2008 to 2% in 2014.

Seattle-based Fred Hutchinson Cancer Research Center provides an on-site nationally accredited child care facility, Hutch Kids Child Care, which admits children from as young as 6 weeks to 5 years old. While the child care facility is open to other children, kids of employees have priority admission and receive a subsidy.

Fred Hutchinson staff scientist Kavita Garg said that having an on-site child care facility at her company ensured she remained in the workforce while she had young children. Garg's daughter started day care from the time she was 11 months old until kindergarten. "It made it much easier to work with the day care right there. I had my first kid when I was a graduate student and I had to work reduced hours as my child was at home with a nanny," she said. With her younger child—the one who eventually was admitted to her employer's day care—Garg said she was initially also thinking of reducing her work hours, as paying for a full-time nanny was working out to be too expensive.

"But with Hutch Kids being right there, I was able to continue with breastfeeding and check on her. I felt comfortable with her being in Hutch Kids instead of [with] a nanny, so for me to actually have my daughter physically there with me was huge," she said. "I would have probably opted out for a few years if I was not satisfied with child care options."

For smaller employers that may not be able to shell out for on-site day care, child care subsidies or pooling with a group of other businesses in the area to build a "joint" day care for employees of several workplaces would be another option.

"Returnships"

One of the most significant employee pools that companies currently overlook are women who want to return to the workforce after an extended leave. At the end of the day, children grow up. Women who may have to take a few months—or even a few years—off should not have to do so at the risk of their careers.

More organizations are picking up on this and now offer "returnships," a term trademarked by Goldman Sachs. These paid return-to-work programs, increasingly being offered by companies like JPMorgan Chase and a small percentage of law firms, make a commitment to train and hire women who return to work after an absence. They have helped highly accomplished women get back to work after leaves, whether they took time off to take care of a child or a sick family member. While "returnships" are often structured like paid internships—where only a small number of participants are made successful job offers after completion—they have helped many women navigate re-entry into the workforce. They help women who may have taken a significant leave of absence—perhaps even more than a decade—bridge that gap back into employability, even if not always with the same company she had the "returnship" with.

A *Harvard Business Review* article explains the successful Goldman Sachs "returnship" program. The bank piloted an eight-week paid internship for men and women who had interrupted their careers in their New York office in 2008. Six out of 11 participants were hired upon completion. Participants were offered "meaty projects" and opportunities to meet senior leadership. The program is now offered in several locations around the world and has helped more than 150 women return to the workforce, according to the company's 2014 Environmental, Social and Governance Impact report.

Other companies are trying to stay ahead of the curve by offering programs that accommodate for employees who may have life events that require them to take long leaves of absence.

Global technology company SAP's chief diversity and inclusion officer Anka Wittenberg shared the key tenets of the company's Stay in Touch program, which helps to retain qualified employees. SAP found that employees often face problems when they return to work after a long absence.

"To strengthen the bond between employees and SAP, minimize costs and ensure that know-how stays within the company, SAP now offers the Stay in Touch program on a global level. Based on successful pilots done in India and Germany, best practices and experiences have been brought together in this global program," according to a fact sheet on the program SAP shared with me.

Some actionable best practices from SAP's policy are outlined below:

- The company and department hold regular meetings and maintain close contact with the employee to share pertinent information during the absence. The program allows employees to ease into their period of absence and helps them to quickly become productive after their return.

- Employees are informed about developments regarding their career options or their line of business in general.

- All employees with a permanent contract, regardless of age or career stage, are eligible for the program for extended absences such as: parental leave for *all* genders; sabbatical; caring for a relative; sickness.

- Participating employees should actively look for a "Stay in Touch" buddy, which is in most cases a team member or a direct colleague who discusses the details of the absence, activities during absence and communication arrangements between the company and employee.

- At least 12 weeks before the employee returns, the following issues should be discussed with the manager: future role of the employee, as well as potential alternatives to her last position; a change of contract, if the employee wishes, such as reduced working hours; possible training or further education.

According to Wittenberg, SAP's return-to-work program has been among the company's most successful initiatives for retaining top female talent.

Where Should Your Company Start?

"Companies are at very different stages in terms of how they can best accommodate for working mothers," said Anna Steffeney, a former IT executive and founder of LeaveLogic, a startup that helps companies implement maternity leave benefits. "Smaller companies should start by looking at whether their paid leave policies are in place at all, while established companies might want to look at expanding existing leave policies and take a look at whether they have off- and on-ramping policies for pregnant women and new mothers," she said.

The difference in policies on this issue by country is also significant. In the U.S., paid leave has become a hot-button topic that features heavily in political campaigns. Indeed, it's devastating that a working mother's career options and her child's care can be determined by how progressive her employer is on this issue. Steffeney remains optimistic about how America can take the lead on the paid leave issue.

"I think there's a perfect storm brewing," said Steffeney. "I think the national conversation has sparked employees to bring these grievances to employers. And there's a social media impact, where employers can't deny that employee expectations have moved."

More companies would benefit from assessing where they stand on supporting employees with children. This is an opportunity for employers to differentiate themselves and innovate early to find solutions. It's good for women, but it's also great for business. And like many conclusions in this book, the most impactful solutions are initiatives and policies that benefit both genders such as paid leave, flexibility and child care support.

5

IMPLICIT BIASES AND MALE DIVERSITY CHAMPIONS

The most progressive companies are focused on advancing women, Jeffery Tobias Halter, president of diversity consultancy YWomen, tells me. "And the ones that are losing are focusing on recruitment of women. Women can come through the door, but they won't stay if you don't find a way to fix culture."

He should know—Halter was one of the men in the unenviable position of leading diversity efforts at The Coca-Cola Company as it recovered from the largest discrimination class action lawsuit in history.

Now, efforts to foster a more collaborative office culture coincide with a time in history when gender, ethnic, racial, religious and sexual diversity is on the rise everywhere. Globally, more women are entering the workforce, more likely to hold at least mid-managerial positions and can often be managing a male employee. While the workplace has evolved significantly, few workplaces are equipped with the knowledge of how to retain more women.

This chapter focuses on inclusion and makes the case for why everyone stands to gain when companies foster effective dialogue about how to make *all* employees successful, regardless of gender, race, sexual orientation or any other factor.

Even if companies embark on these initiatives to better gender diversity, there's ample evidence to show that championing even one "type" of inclusiveness is likely to empower other discriminated individuals too. It's a tough task to undertake, perhaps the most difficult initiative when it comes to championing diversity. This is one that requires cultures and mindsets to shift—no easy feat.

Is There A Business Case For Bias Training?

Refusing to tackle the "diversity question" head on could potentially cost U.S. employers over $64 billion in turnover, annually.

That's according to data from the Corporate Leavers Survey, which found that annually, over 2 million professionals in the U.S. voluntarily leave their jobs solely because of unfairness. Other findings include:

- Compared with heterosexual, Caucasian men, employees of color are three times more likely to leave solely because they felt they were treated unfairly.

- Respondents who cited unfairness as the sole reason for leaving were most likely to mention the following instances of unfair conduct: *"(1) Being asked to attend more recruiting or community-related events than others because of one's race, gender, religion or sexual orientation, (2) being passed over for a promotion due to one's personal characteristics, (3) being publicly humiliated."*

- Twenty-seven percent of those who experienced unfairness said that their workplace experiences "strongly discouraged them from recommending their employer to other potential employees," and 13% of respondents felt that the unfairness "strongly discouraged them from recommending their employer's products or services to others."

Women Who Speak

Many of the gender biases that crop up at the workplace today relate to traditional gender role expectations. For example, women are expected to be docile, "feminine" and less vocal than men.

As such, women often face a double bind when they speak up at work. If they do speak up, they're often interrupted or considered too aggressive. When they opt to stay quiet, they're seen as having fewer leadership qualities or even incompetent. I'll explore this concept further in a future chapter on advancing women into leadership roles.

In one experiment by Yale psychologist Victoria L. Brescoll, male and female professionals were asked to gauge the competence of chief executives who spoke more or less frequently. Male CEOs who shared their opinions more than their peers were rewarded with 10% higher ratings of competence. By contrast, female CEOs who spoke up more than their peers were given 14% lower ratings by both genders.

Implicit biases—the ones we can't easily identify— inform some of the most pressing decisions at work, such as how much to compensate, who to promote and whose feedback to take into consideration. Smart organizations will recognize a need to frame these biases and find ways to change the culture to be more inclusive.

Google's Example

Innovative companies are using data in an attempt to inform their employees about biases.

Brian Welle, a research scientist at Google, was tasked with researching hidden biases in the workplace. The resulting 90-minute lecture uses data to back up the uncomfortable truth that everybody is, in fact, a little bit racist or sexist. Welle then explains how the most harmful damage can often be done through unconscious biases, when people don't mean to inflict harm or can't even identify how their biases manifest in their personal preferences.

He mentions a computer simulation that demonstrated how a systematic 1% bias against women in performance evaluations can work its way through the ranks, leading to the paltry representation of women in management.

"You can think of this as women receiving a performance score from 1 to 100 and men receiving a performance score from 1 to 101. ... One percentage of bias (against women) in the performance score ends up skewing the distribution of women at the top to 35% of women at the very top of the organization. ... This exact same pyramidal structure is what we see in corporate America. Almost any single organization you go to, you will see a skew against women at the very top."

While this skew isn't purely because of bias, Welle says it would be "naïve" to say bias doesn't play any part in hampering women's advancement.

Welle's research concludes with good news, however. Science says we can condition ourselves to recognize these biases, and as we become more aware of how these unconscious preferences influence our decision-making, the higher chance we have of trying to get others to confront them too.

The video has some fascinating insights and would be worth organizing a "brown bag" lunch for employees at your organization to watch together. Diversity initiatives don't always have to cost money or take a whole lot of time to get started on.

A Free Bias Test For Employees

Highlighting existing biases is a good start to strategizing how to best manage them. Even people who work in diversity within their organization will have implicit biases that were formed by culture, upbringing, parents, education and a whole other range of factors.

It takes little effort to complete these series of Implicit Association Tests, but the results are well worth taking note of. I was surprised when I took the test; when presented with words like "marriage" and "family," my brain immediately gravitated towards the word "female," while words like "career" and "salary" paired up with "male."

Leaders must recognize that, by and large, their employees will not be explicitly biased or discriminatory. It's often a series of behaviors within the organization that accumulate—off-color jokes, women consistently being interrupted or just a dominant, hierarchical culture of leadership—that create systemic barriers to women's advancement.

Solutions To Unspeakable Problems

Diversity consultant Cook Ross Inc. produced a written guide on how to combat hidden bias. Although the guide is from 2008, it still bears relevance on recommendations for leaders to manage implicit biases. I have included a few pointers below:

- *"Reframe the conversation to focus on fair treatment and respect, and away from discrimination and 'protected classes.' Review every aspect of the employment life cycle for hidden bias—screening resumes, interviews, onboarding, assignment process, mentoring programs, performance evaluation, identifying high performers, promotion and termination.*

- *Ensure that anonymous employee surveys are conducted company-wide to first understand what specific issues of hidden bias and unfairness might exist at your workplace. Each department or location may have different issues.*

- *Conduct anonymous surveys with former employees to understand what were the issues they faced, what steps could be taken for them to consider coming back, whether they encourage or discourage prospective employees from applying for positions at your company and whether they encourage or discourage prospective customers/clients from using your company's products or services.*

- *Offer customized training based upon survey results of current and former employees that includes examples of hidden bias, forms of unfairness that are hurtful and demotivating, and positive methods to discuss these issues."*

The guide also states that some companies choose to undergo an organizational diversity audit.

The Results Of Implicit Bias Training At Google

Can making employees aware of their implicit biases directly change company culture? It's too early to tell. Admittedly, the results will have to be measured over a longer term, with regular measures on whether bias and unfairness are a widespread issue at your company. Even companies that are actively working on changing biases— Google, for example—haven't solved the problem. At Google, only 30% of employees are female, with 21% in senior leadership and a severe underrepresentation of female engineers. But ignoring institutional and cultural blocks to women's growth is also not the answer.

Google offered *The New York Times* several anecdotes that seem to indicate a less biased culture as a result of its "hidden prejudices" training.

According to the article, Google opened a new building where "someone spotted the fact that all the conference rooms were named after male scientists; in the past, that might have gone unmentioned, but this time the names were changed."

In another case, a male manager attended a meeting where he and his colleagues were deciding whether or not to promote a female engineer. Because he had been through the bias training, he was aware that, as males, they wouldn't be able to fully understand what a woman engineer could bring to the table. "Just raising the awareness was enough for people to think about it," Laszlo Bock, Google's SVP of people operations, said in the article. The group decided to promote the woman.

"Mr. Bock saw all of these actions as evidence that the training was working," the article reports.

An Inclusion Checklist At Meetings

Leaders at other technology company are also exploring ways to make inclusion more pervasive. Red Hat, a software provider, rates highly on Glassdoor.com, an independent website where current and former employees can anonymously review their employers. Among positive feedback on company culture and innovation, the words "flexibility" and "progressive" featured highly in reviews.

Inclusiveness doesn't happen by accident, the company's chief people officer DeLisa Alexander tells me. I obtained the company's "Inclusion Champion Support"— a one-page document that explicitly lays out a plan to include everyone in meetings. Alexander's leadership team is piloting the approach, which they learned from Stanford University's Clayman Institute, and she has shared the tips with all of Red Hat's employees in an internal blog.

When managers are made more aware about how some employees may not be comfortable speaking up, they're equipped with prompts to encourage participation from everyone, she tells me. Sometimes a soft nudge that your opinion matters is all it takes, particularly if you're the only woman, or minority, in the room.

Excerpts from the checklist, provided by Red Hat, are below:

1. SHARE THE AIRTIME

"Action: Keep track of who is speaking in the meeting."

The document includes the names of all attendees of the meeting and a checklist to keep track of who speaks in the meeting.

"Action: Invite input from quiet individuals and those on the phone."

The checklist advises leaders to create opportunities for quiet individuals to speak up and contribute. "Highlight the knowledge and insight they bring to the table."

The document also provides scripts so that meeting leaders can easily facilitate more participation:

"I'm eager to hear your thoughts, _____. You have experience in this area; I'm curious what you think about this plan."

"_____, you often notice things that others don't. What are we missing?"

Regardless of industry, a much lesser proportion of women share their opinions or raise their voices at work when compared to men. Making meeting leaders aware of this fact can be useful to counter this.

2. INTERRUPT THE INTERRUPTERS

"Action: Ensure that speakers are able to finish their thought by saying:

'_____, please hold your comments. I'd like to hear the rest of what _____ has to say before we move on."

'Wait a moment, I'm interested in what _____ was saying about this. (Please, continue.)'"

Again, Red Hat's list gets to the heart of a major problem in the corporate world today—when women share ideas, they're often interrupted, ignored or even chastised by men and other senior women for speaking up.

3. MAKE EFFECTIVE INTRODUCTIONS

"Action: Make space for others to contribute by introducing them in a powerful way.

The way you introduce people conveys information about their performance and contributions. Take the time to highlight their strengths and accomplishments, and how others might benefit from getting to know them better:

'This is _____. He's been a great partner to me on our cross-functional projects, he's very skilled at navigating difficult conversations and pulling in the business perspective ...'

'This is _____. I've been wanting to introduce the two of you, because she heads up sales in your region, and in fact, she's surpassed her sales quota by a wide margin two quarters in a row.'"

4. SEEK FIRST TO UNDERSTAND, THEN TO BE UNDERSTOOD

"Action: Listen with the intent to understand and ask clarifying questions from the speaker's story or presentation (not from an autobiographical lens).

'When you mentioned _____, what does that look like?'

'Can you help me understand what you meant when you said _____?'"

"In my opinion, bias training alone isn't sufficient. It's important to pair bias training with processes that help us overcome the bias," says Alexander.

Inclusion As A Leadership Style

Fostering inclusion that becomes part of company culture is always a top-down measure. When leaders prioritize diversity, research shows it benefits their own careers too— inclusion is actually a highly regarded leadership trait. A Catalyst study, which delved into attitudes about what makes a great leader across six countries, found one common theme—inclusion is key.

Highlights from research in the six countries include:
- *"The more included employees felt, the more innovative they reported being in their jobs.*

- *The more included employees felt, the more they reported engaging in team citizenship behaviors— going above and beyond the 'call of duty' to help other team members and meet workgroup objectives.*

- *Perceiving similarities with co-workers engendered a feeling of belongingness, while perceiving differences led to feelings of uniqueness."*

Catalyst also provides a handy, free-of-charge quiz that managers could benefit from taking. The quiz can help leaders understand whether their organizations are inclusive and what areas need to be improved.

Engaging Men To Change The Conversation

YWomen's Halter says the other key component to changing culture is engaging men.

"You're not going to drive systemic change without male engagement. If you look at corporate America today, depending where you are, 80 to 85% of senior leadership is made up of white men," he tells me.

While Halter conducts formal training to equip male advocates to champion gender diversity, he says engaging men within organizations doesn't have to be a lengthy or costly process.

1. Get male leaders to attend women's conferences.
One technique is to encourage male senior leaders to attend women's leadership conferences.

"What works is this notion of active immersion," he says. "Suddenly, you put a man in a situation where he's among two or three thousand women and that energy can be both electrifying and scary," he says. "It's the first time many men have experienced something like it."

But what often results, according to him, is that leaders are able to "step back and feel the energy and ask themselves, 'How do we harness this in our organization?'" Men who attend women's leadership conferences start to realize the conversations are rarely around "fluffy feminine things" but about business processes and the bottom line. It builds respect and a deeper understanding of women's experiences at the workplace and how they differ from a man's experience.

2. Identify the champions.

Halter, who has worked with organizations like Procter & Gamble and General Electric, says engaging men as diversity champions can be challenging, as in any given organization, there are only about 20% of men actively willing to advocate for women.

"Often they don't know what to do. Senior leaders have conceptualized the idea but don't know what it's like on a day-to-day basis." As a result, companies invest only in what Halter calls the "fix the woman model," which focuses on training, coaching and developing high-potential women. But they miss the opportunity to coach and hold men accountable too. That's where creating a support network of male champions can be a game-changer.

Most importantly, find male volunteers who opt in to fostering inclusion. Halter calls these men "the early adapters"—cohorts of men within an organization who believe in the need to champion more women leaders. Once a group has been organized, the business case for diversity must be emphasized.

"Once you link the reason for engaging male advocates to the bottom-line impact of diversity, it's easier to lay out a strategy with metrics," he says.

3. Create a safe space to ask tough questions.

Part of Halter's training involves 10-on-one workshops with men, but also bringing in a "cultural coach" who is often a female diversity expert willing to answer questions from a woman's perspective at work.

He says conversations between men and the cultural coach range from the leadership competencies that men value versus women, to questions about what constitutes sexual harassment. But the conversations are always honest and non-judgmental.

Here, the "training" aspect is of less focus; instead the idea is to encourage active discussion around the barriers to women's advancement in each organization and how men can help move the needle.

Again, simple awareness and empathy-building can lead to more male leaders advocating for women on their teams and changing persistent expectations about what constitutes a "woman's job."

For example, Virgin Group founder and billionaire Richard Branson recently made a simple observation—that women took more notes than men in meetings, a carry-over from the expectation that women should do the support work. His advice? "To counteract the gender bias, men shouldn't take over the note-taking from women, everyone should be taking notes!"

How Engaging Men To Champion Diversity Empowers Them

Male participation in advancing women makes sense for a variety of reasons. Cultural change starts at the top and most leaders continue to be male, so by default their engagement is crucial. But in recent times, expecting a more inclusive and gender-balanced workforce is driving male employee engagement too.

Catalyst SVP of research Jeanine Prime says that more male employees she interviews cite their own benefits as a reason to be engaged in gender issues.

"Many of the men I speak to recognize that traditional workplaces are set up with restrictive models where men are earners and have a wife at home to raise children and take care of personal affairs. But those norms of work and family are beginning to change around the globe," she says. This idea of career success rails against the expectations that many men have of the workplace today, where work-life balance and equal parenting are starting to become more important to men.

"It's often a light bulb that goes off when they find traditional gender norms at work too restrictive, a command-and-control leadership style too oppressive, and that's when we find men really wanting to foster organizational change."

Cultural change—doing away with hidden biases and truly engaging men to champion for women—won't happen overnight. But with a strategy in place, innovative organizations will continue to make inclusion a business priority.

6

OVERCOMING THE "OLD BOYS' CLUB"—

WOMEN'S NETWORKS AND SPONSORSHIP

More women than ever before are entering the workforce through entry-level positions in corporations around the world. In the U.S., more women are likely to graduate from college and make up nearly half the country's workforce. But somewhere along the pipeline, women get stuck in jobs that pay less than their male counterparts, or in positions that have significantly less influence than men who graduated with the same qualifications. A McKinsey study found that 62% of women in corporate America are in staff jobs, or jobs that do not lead directly to the C-suite. In contrast, only 41% to 48% of men are in staff jobs.

A large part of why women often drop out of the workforce lies in the retention challenges explored in previous chapters. So far, this book has focused on strategies to attract and keep talented women in corporate jobs. But once you have that critical mass of women in middle-management, how many actually make it to executive positions? The statistics are bleak; in the United States, over 60% of women in Top 500 companies begin their careers in line roles that directly impact the bottom line, not support-staff roles. Yet the figures at the top are exactly the opposite: About two-thirds of the women in executive positions are in human resources, marketing or other support functions.

Several cultural and institutional factors have consistently resulted in qualified, ambitious women getting stuck in support-staff jobs or "pink ghettos," a term coined in the 1980s to describe female-dominated jobs.

The corporate conversation is rightfully moving away from simply upping the numbers of female employees to a more nuanced debate about what it takes to get more women into business-critical, decision-making leadership positions.

Even women who are able to find the domestic and organization support they need to stay on at work during their childbearing years still face challenges in getting to senior leadership roles that lead anywhere near the C-suite. Many get "mommy tracked," where corporate misperceptions about their availability and commitment to work lead to a gradual decrease in responsibilities and soon enough, a decrease in leadership opportunities. Women are also routinely excluded from the informal networks that are crucial to succeeding in the corporate structure, especially when they have family commitments.

The lack of access to the traditionally male-dominated "insider" network that still lines the top of most corporate environments is hurting women's advancement. Becky Blalock, former chief information officer of Southern Company and the first woman in that company's C-suite, tells me that women are often passed over for jobs they are fully ready and qualified for "because they're not invited to informal networks." Blalock recalls confronting a male boss; in the four years she worked under him, he had never once taken her to lunch, despite socializing with other male colleagues.

"He protested that he never 'took' out those colleagues for lunch, but the fact is, even when they went for an informal meal, my male colleagues were getting face time with the boss that I was entirely missing out on. These informal lunches eventually played out in these male peers getting the important assignments and promotions, while I was being excluded," she says.

"Fortunately, my boss listened and realized what I was saying," she says. "But most women wouldn't go up and say something and most men wouldn't even realize they're cutting women out from these very important informal networks."

A few recent sex discrimination lawsuits in the U.S. point to a reality I've heard time and again while covering women's leadership—how men and women's advancement opportunities are unequal, largely due to how top jobs are often decided over rounds of golf and late-night drinks.

Take the landmark Ellen Pao case that was decided in March 2015—Pao sued her employer, the venture capital firm Kleiner Perkins, for gender discrimination, claiming she was repeatedly passed over for promotions, denied access to the company's "old boys' club" and subjected to inappropriate behavior. While Pao lost the case, it generated a media maelstrom around how covert gender bias is actually rampant in many organizations. Another tech giant, Twitter, is also under scrutiny for gender equality, and a former employee alleges the company's leadership was:

- *"Effectively discouraging women from seeking or applying for senior-level and leadership positions.*
- *Failing and refusing to consider women for promotion on the same basis as men are considered.*

- *Providing women employees interested in promotion shifting, inconsistent and inaccurate statements about the requirements and qualifications necessary for promotion."*

A Gallup poll found that 15% of U.S. career women expressed feeling passed over for a promotion or opportunity at work because of their gender. The results were roughly similar when accounting for age, education and type of employment. A separate Catalyst study states that men get more career-making leadership roles than equally qualified and motivated women. Further, the study found that when women used the same strategies as men to get ahead, they still advanced less than their male peers and lagged in pay growth.

While the majority of organizations point to the lack of qualified women in the talent pool, another "fix the women" explanation, forward-thinking companies have been testing a variety of strategies to help identify and advance high-potential women, such as building a robust women's network and building sponsorship opportunities.

For purposes of clarity, leadership roles in this context refer to roles above "manager" level that lead to the C-suite, if we define the corporate ladder as:

1. Entry-Level
2. Manager
3. Director
4. Vice President
5. Senior Vice President
6. C-suite

The goal is to get more women into senior VP and C-suite roles, where they are typically least represented in corporate organizations globally.

Again, these two strategies to foster diversity and inclusion must be driven from the top down. It is the only way to ensure that these efforts to develop and accelerate more women are sustainable and successful.

Women's Networks

Women's networks within companies have long suffered a bad reputation—with good reason, when the networks are treated more like social gatherings; think book clubs and low budget with few female employees acting as volunteers over and above their daily responsibilities. Leaders—male or female—never make an appearance, and soon, the network becomes a place where entry- and middle-management-level women get together to socialize but don't have a business objective.

Research finds that those are the types of networks that do not help advance women in any way, as they don't serve as a way to penetrate the "old boys' club" I mentioned in the last chapter. In contrast, the most successful women's networks have CEO buy-in, a strong steering committee and agenda, with gatherings that inform and educate, as much as they become a forum for female employees to network and learn from each other. The network becomes a valuable resource to identify high-potential women who are given equal consideration for top assignments and promotion opportunities.

A recent KPMG study on women's leadership found that nine in 10 working women believe that their own drive will accelerate their path to leadership. But the majority also agreed that interactions with other women—colleagues, role models and professional networks—play a key role in advancing women. The most significant leadership lessons were learned from other female colleagues, reported two-thirds of respondents. A majority (82%) believe in career advancement by having access to and networking with women leaders.

"Implementing leadership programs that develop and connect high-potential women with senior leaders may be key to helping more women advance," the report states.

A separate *Harvard Business Review* article also finds that a successful corporate women's network can help female employees develop leadership capabilities that can be business-critical.

"Creating a safe setting—a coaching relationship, a women's leadership program, a support group of peers—in which women can interpret these messages is critical to their leadership identity development."

Fortunately, women's networks can often be a great business investment too. Research from the Financial Women's Association (FWA) found that affinity networks have a positive impact on a company's bottom line, and successful networks generate ideas that are connected to business returns. According to the survey, 39% of women say their firm's women's network is a factor in staying with the company.

A women's network doesn't need to be cost- or time-intensive. But it must absolutely be linked to business goals, with senior-level buy-in, according to the various companies I've talked to around the world on building robust corporate women's networks. I've outlined some best practices for successful corporate women's networks below, with input from leaders at Deloitte, Sodexo and SAP.

1. Tie in the network to the business case.

For an affinity group to have sufficient resources and commitment, its objectives must be clearly stated and tied to business goals. Deloitte LLP launched its Women's Initiative Network (WIN) in 1993, spurred by the goal to retain more female employees and promote more women to partners. WIN has since taken on a life of its own, sparking worldwide women's conferences, workshops and a wealth of resources for female employees.

The business case for starting the network? Getting more women to stay and succeed at Deloitte. In 1993, 7% of the firm's partners were female but current levels are at about three times those numbers. In early 2015, Deloitte LLP became the first of the Big Four accounting firms to elect its first female CEO, Cathy Engelbert (U.S.). A separate Deloitte publication stated that its Women as Buyers program—which helps Deloitte professionals understand how women executives make corporate buying decisions—generated more than $750 million in revenue over three years. The program was born out of the company's WIN network.

With the creation of WIN, Deloitte created a tangible set of diversity metrics to aim for, complete with an external diversity advisory board that was once led by the late Sally Ride, the first American woman in space.

2. Get CEO buy-in and senior leadership visibility.

Deloitte's WIN network is accountable to the firm's CEO, not human resources. This means the network is recognized as a business strategy, not an HR one. Ensuring senior leaders are plugged into the agenda of the network ensures it is not a random, haphazard project, but a sustainable business goal to engage and advance female employees.

Top leaders within the organization—and, where possible, inspirational leaders from outside the corporation—should be brought in to regularly address the women's network. Senior female leaders within the company should ideally be a part of the network. Again, the company must position the network as a valuable business imperative, not a social gathering. More senior women are likely to make time if they see the value added of being engaged; they may enjoy even greater visibility within the organization for being involved in a high-quality business network, not a token "diversity obligation." Senior male employees should also be heavily involved in championing the value of the network.

3. Have a clear plan.

"These employee resource groups can play a critical role in engaging high-potential female employees," Catalyst research director Anna Beninger tells me. "When junior women see senior women front and center, they picture themselves there, it can be hugely beneficial to their career trajectory in the long term." Women's networks should have a good mix of idea-sharing from internal and external leaders, with actionable agendas on equipping women to advance at your company. FWA research found that women's networks fall short in making the connections that matter to pay, new business growth and external networking. Women were also more interested in education relating to career growth than personal topics, with particular interest in new work and career skills (such as new software and social media) and trending technology, according to the report.

Ideally, regular meetings should take place, but with technology, it doesn't always have to be a physical meeting.

I've heard differing points of view on whether men should be regular participants in these groups. Opponents say women should be allowed to have a safe male-free space to share information and ideas. Proponents say educating men through these networks on the experience of their female peers is necessary for engaging men in diversity. Each company's diversity and inclusion priorities will be different, depending on size, industry and even who is in the driver's seat.

There's only one constant among successful corporate women's networks—they are all mandated from the top, with a clear business goal in mind. No matter the size, budget and structure of a women's network, it is never a mysterious, informal concept where women just "hang out in a conference room over lunch."

Beyond Mentorship: The Case For Sponsorship

The oft-repeated wisdom of finding the right mentor to ensure women's advancement comes up for career women more than I would like to admit. The "fix women" camp lays out much advice for women on how to find a mentor—look for someone who looks different than you, don't call this person a "mentor"—right down to how often a woman should approach her mentor.

Can a mentoring relationship, no matter how powerful, really accelerate a woman's career? Are women lacking mentors? Actually, no. When it comes to mentoring, 83% of women report having at least one mentor in their careers, compared with 76% of men. In fact, 21% of women report having four or more mentors, whereas just 15% of men report having that many.

Instead, men are 46% more likely to have sponsors—advocates for their advancement within the organization—than women. And some experts link the low representation of women and minority men in top corporate jobs on the lack of access they have to senior-level sponsors. More organizations—American Express, IBM and PricewaterhouseCoopers, for example—are exploring innovative ways to ensure more women get direct access to the mostly male leaders at their organizations.

Research shows informal mentoring—where mentors are casual listeners or a shoulder to lean on—doesn't lead to more advancement opportunities for women. Most informal mentors do not have the level of influence on the woman's career that will directly lead to her promotion. Instead, companies would benefit from developing a sponsorship program to help propel more female employees into leadership.

The data set on sponsorship is small; few companies have a formal sponsorship program with data that stretches far enough to conclusively tie these programs with an increase in women leaders. But sponsorship does offer an actionable solution to widening the networks so that women have a better chance of accessing "the old boys' club" that still dominates most industries. By facilitating regular meetings between senior leaders and high-potential women deliberately and strategically, companies have a higher chance of bridging the gap between female middle-managers and the decision-makers who recruit for leadership roles. Early successes at some large companies are also promising.

Sponsors are allies in a woman's current company who will use their influence to advocate for her at the decision-making table to fill large, visible projects and promotions. Catalyst research finds that the more senior your sponsor, the faster the advancement opportunities for the protégé. If we think of mentors as career developers, sponsors are the equivalent of career accelerators.

Benefits to the protégé may seem obvious; a senior leader will advocate for her success, her skills and increase her visibility and access to plum assignments. But there's actually evidence that even the sponsor—the senior leader— and the organization, as a whole, significantly benefit from sponsoring women.

Catalyst research states:

"A protégé's career is clearly enhanced by a good relationship with a sponsor. But sponsors benefit too—by establishing reputations as discerning leaders invested in talent sustainability, as powerful contributors to their organization's success, by learning from employees at every level, and gaining leadership skills that can further enhance their own careers. Sponsorship benefits companies by creating more effective and committed teams and fostering a 'pay it forward' mentality that makes employees feel valued and supported."

I interviewed Sylvia Ann Hewlett, CEO of the Center for Talent Innovation and one of the most vocal advocates for sponsorship through her book *Forget a Mentor, Find a Sponsor*. In an email interview with me, Hewlett says more companies can make women's sponsorship a priority quickly and cost-effectively.

How can organizations build an effective sponsorship program for women?

Sylvia Ann Hewlett: "It's important to not force the relationship. Directors can't say to their executive team, 'Go pick a woman and sponsor her.' It has to be organic. So what companies are doing very successfully is making both sides of the equation aware of how powerful this relationship can be and they are creating 'pathways' for sponsorship.

An example: At Morgan Stanley, newly minted female managing directors never met the very senior guys, because there were no women at the top to speak of and there was no natural way of connecting. So the company put on a breakfast every month that was very carefully planned. They invited their senior leaders and the newly promoted class of female managing directors (which was exactly the level where they tended to lose women). They seated them cleverly, made sure the women gave some of the presentations, and sponsorship flourished. They just needed a venue to showcase each other's abilities."

What's your advice for smaller companies that may not want to spend much, on how to structure sponsorship?

Sylvia Ann Hewlett: "Smaller companies have the advantage of having close-knit teams who likely all know one another and constantly work together. This environment presents many opportunities for sponsorship to grow organically, as most team members are in the direct line of sight of a potential sponsor. As sponsor/protégé relationships are developed organically, creating opportunities for sponsorship need not be a huge monetary commitment. An organization should consider hosting organized and purposeful meetings or events during which junior team members can shine. One example is a regular company brainstorm in which junior team members are tasked with helping leadership work through an actual business challenge."

How does sponsorship impact the bottom line?

Sylvia Ann Hewlett: "Sponsorship translates into quantifiable career traction. When it comes to asking for a pay raise, the majority of women (70%) resist confronting their boss, but with a sponsor in their corner, 38% of women summon the courage to negotiate their salaries. Women with sponsors are also 22% more likely to request getting assigned to a high-visibility team or plum project. And 68% of fully-sponsored women feel they are progressing through the ranks at a satisfactory pace. Those numbers result in female employees who are more engaged and more likely to attract similar talent. The high levels of commitment and engagement will improve the bottom line of a company."

Catalyst director Beninger says sponsorship can even bring a monetary boost for the senior leaders—Catalyst research showed managers who sponsored protégés had an average of $25,075 greater pay growth from 2008 to 2010. "Our research shows if you pay it forward, it pays back. Sponsors become recognized in the organization as leaders who nurture talent to become future leaders."

Sponsorship is not a new concept, Beninger says. Many men get access to advancement opportunities, simply by connecting with (mostly male) senior leaders naturally. "Most sponsorship happens behind closed doors and women are often excluded," she adds. Like in Blalock's example, it can start out as harmless as her boss having a casual lunch with her male peers, but eventually that face time builds up.

"Senior-level men will generally only sponsor junior-level men, if you don't have a formal program," Beninger adds. It can be uncomfortable or unnatural for senior men to meet junior women at the organization. "But with a sponsorship initiative, you remove the perceived discomfort around senior male leaders meeting with junior female employees because people are given a reason to meet during work times."

A Sponsorship Program That Works

A *Harvard Business Review* article lays out six tips on creating a formal corporate program that is successful.

Set clear objectives of the program.
Some programs try to incorporate both mentoring and sponsoring into the same program. This is a mistake, as they're both significant undertakings. Instead, your program must state clear objectives.

Select and match sponsors and protégés accordingly.
If you're trying to achieve career advancement for protégés, match them with a sponsor who holds a power position that would make the difference. When matching for personal growth, it's more important that both parties get along well to ensure regular contact.

Keep direct supervisors in the loop.
Any centrally run programs that do not involve the protégé's direct boss signal that diversity is a HR "problem." Direct managers should have buy-in.

The article points to a Deutsche Bank sponsorship program for female managing directors, which also involves leadership evaluations, external coaches and leadership workshops.

Create training around gender and leadership.
It's a mistake to assume highly talented employees will naturally understand the complexities of gender and leadership. Matching a junior woman with a senior male without any training around gender or leadership could create misunderstandings. It will also help sponsors understand if there are specific challenges that high-potential women face that perhaps star male employees may not understand. "The strategies and tactics that helped the men progress in their careers may not be appealing or even feasible for the women," the article states.

A good example is how men and women are judged when they develop the same leadership traits. The same things that are considered leadership potential for men— speaking in a commanding tone, for example—are rarely as effective for women. As previously highlighted, gender stereotypes and unconscious biases play a role in determining how effective a woman is as a leader.

The *HBR* article mentions Sodexo's mentoring program, which it claims helps senior leaders understand their own unconscious biases when they sponsor women. As a result, they also become diversity champions.

A continuation of the *HBR* article:

Hold sponsors accountable.
To run a truly effective sponsorship program, companies must hold sponsors accountable. The article points to a program at IBM Europe, where sponsors are tasked with ensuring that high-potential women become promotable within a year. As a result, the sponsors use their political profile to raise these women's profiles within the company and to get them involved in highly visible projects. At the

end of the year, if the woman is not promoted, it is considered a failure of the sponsor—not the woman.

Ensure sustained contact with protégés.
Because sponsorship programs are set for a fixed term, once protégés have reached their goal—a promotion or a highly visible role—sponsors move on. Instead, participants should be supported way past just a set destination, especially as they may require extra support during the critical first 100 days in a new role. The article states that this extra attention could lead to not only promotions but also strong, long-lasting transitions.

I met Jane (name has been changed to protect her identity), a director at a large multinational company, through a mutual friend. When I mentioned my research around sponsorship to her, her eyes sparkled; the words energized her. While not authorized to speak to the media by her company, I couldn't get Jane's enthusiasm out of my mind.

She proudly showed me a box that was given to her by a male senior executive at her company five years ago. In it was a button that said, "It Takes One." The token was a part of the company's formal sponsorship program, where senior leaders in the corporate women's network were encouraged to identify and sponsor one high-potential woman. The senior executive had worked with Jane before, but had been in a different business line.

While Jane says she had "always been a high performer and leaned in," being sponsored gave her a much-needed boost to her career. "It indicated to me that a senior leader was willing to use his political capital to advocate for my success," she says. Sponsorship entailed regular meetings between protégé and sponsor, where she could discuss her career. The sponsor was also crucial in advocating for her during the company's annual promotion meeting, where a team of executives—not a single line manager—gather to discuss how promotions would be awarded.

A year after being selected for sponsorship, Jane was promoted to director. She still keeps in regular touch with her sponsor, and since her promotion, has worked more closely with him on business-critical projects.

"It really does take just one to advocate for women's leadership," Jane tells me. "There's nothing nefarious going on; it's not that women are purposely being passed over for leadership roles, but a sponsorship program makes all those at the decision-making table stop and think about the diversity of candidates being considered for leadership roles." As for the male sponsor? He was recently promoted to CFO of the company's U.S. operations.

Sponsorship At SAP

SAP's chief inclusion officer Anka Wittenberg tells me early sponsorship programs at the company have fared particularly well in developing diverse leaders.

One such program takes place at a three-day leadership class, where the top 300 managers at the company are asked to develop two managers each. "We know the studies: Sponsorship drives employee engagement and customer satisfaction." The managers receive training on how to identify and boost these diverse managers.

Sponsorship also features as a key pillar of the company's landmark Leadership Excellence Acceleration Program (LEAP), a 12-month leadership development program that targets talented females who have been identified as high-potential leaders.

"One big part of LEAP is to give visibility to more women," says Wittenberg. The program, which piloted in 2013 in SAP's North America operations, had "great key performance indicators," she says. Out of 50 women who entered the program, 26% applied to higher-level positions after completing the program and 80% got those new jobs, largely due to greater visibility and networking within the organization. "We found 90% of women had face-to-face engagement with recruiting and over 25 executives were involved in the program." The company intends to have a global rollout of the LEAP program.

Wittenberg says sponsorship ties in heavily with a business goal the company set for itself in 2011—to have 25% female leadership by 2017. "It's a big issue as a technology company to attract and advance women," she says. "We are heavily focused on creating an inclusive environment, not only by gender but by generation, cultures, differently abled individuals." A separate but impressive inclusion strategy includes the goal of having 1% of its global workforce comprised of employees with autism by the year 2020.

Every leader I spoke to—on and off the record—for this book repeatedly emphasized how critical senior leadership buy-in is for successful and sustainable inclusion.

For a sponsorship program to truly work, Catalyst's Beninger says the program must be driven from the top down, with tangible involvement from the organization's most senior leaders.

"The crucial outcome is defined as advancement of protégés; the goal is more women get visibility," she says. According to Beninger, who leads Catalyst research on developing high-potential female leaders, it doesn't take a lot of money to have an effective sponsorship program, but it requires time—the time for people to meet and organize. A program that pairs sponsors with protégés for one hour once a month can be very effective, Beninger says.

Sponsorship At Sodexo

Sodexo, the French food services and facilities management multinational corporation, employs close to 420,000 people around the world. The company has been recognized for its diversity practices many times. In a recent study, the company studied 50,000 managers at 90 sites around the world. They found that when there is effective gender balance in management, employee engagement is up and the company enjoys a stronger brand image. In addition, according to a Sodexo newsletter, titled "Gender Balance Business News," "Entities with gender-balanced management were 23% more likely to show an increase in gross profit over the past three consecutive years" and "13% more likely to show consistent organic growth over the past three years."

Rohini Anand, Sodexo's global chief diversity officer, says the metrics of the study confirmed the business case for the company's existing focus on diversity, while helping to drive the business case for sponsoring more talented female employees to advance.

"We have a strong mentoring initiative and we found we need to combine with advocacy and sponsorship," Anand tells me.

Sponsorship has always existed in the fabric of Sodexo. The company regularly has talent discussions around how managers can decide who to sponsor—who are the employees they want to make visible to the organization, she says. "As we have talent discussions, we identify women and minorities we think are worthy of sponsorship based on their performance ... and those individuals are presented to senior leaders. We are putting some process around it now, because the default is to sponsor someone like you," she says.

She points to the company's reciprocal-mentorship program, which is a world apart from the informal mentoring relationships I mentioned previously. In Sodexo's program, 300 participants are matched up across cultures, gender and business lines. "The objective of the program is to match the areas of the mentees' growth with mentors' strength."

"We realized that the promotion rate for mentees who had gone through the program was much higher than the cohort population," Anand tells me. Combined with other informal programs, such as mentoring circles, Anand says the company has worked tirelessly to build a culture of mentorship and development throughout the organization.

Her key takeaways from the success of Sodexo's development programs for women:

1. Hold managers accountable.
Anand says when looking at any program or initiative, it's critical to know *what* you're trying to achieve. Sodexo's mentoring initiatives were created to retain and advance more women, she says. When the objectives and outcomes are clearly defined, it's harder to shift blame. "Metrics without accountability is not effective. In addition to clear metrics to address the outcome we are trying to achieve, we

also hold managers accountable through a link to performance reviews and incentive plans."

2. Establish clear metrics.

"You have to measure what you're doing. Our metrics is what distinguishes this program from any other. We have a robust scorecard that we can keep going back to, to track how we're doing in recruiting, retaining and promoting women and minorities."

3. Ensure you have leadership support.

Position sponsorship/mentorship as a culture change effort and an overall business growth strategy. Ensure you have buy-in from leadership, she says.

If you track the career trajectory of long-standing employees, there's a high chance that who they knew had a huge impact on where they landed up in the organization. Having more women leaders right at the top, as my next two chapters describe, will likely have the unintended outcome of bringing in even more women in coming years. Conversely, an all-male management team will likely continue developing more men to progress within the organization.

While the business case for diversity is clear, it's still tough to practice in reality. At the end of the day, humans are most comfortable associating with and advocating for individuals who look most like them. Without the assistance of the company in making these connections, it's rare they would happen by chance. Senior leaders must recognize and accept this facet of human behavior and identify ways to connect more women with influential individuals within the company. An organization-wide initiative like sponsorship gets more employees taking action to advance diverse employees. Again, to be successful, the efforts must be top down and infiltrate the company culture at every level.

Here's the good news—advocating for high-potential women is not just good for employee morale; it's good for business too. A 2015 McKinsey report I cited previously found a positive correlation between high numbers of female leaders and a company's financial outperformance compared with industry peers globally. "More diverse companies, we believe, are better able to win top talent and improve their customer orientation, employee satisfaction and decision-making, and all that leads to a virtuous cycle of increasing returns," wrote the report's authors.

7

PROPELLING WOMEN TO SENIOR EXECUTIVE POSITIONS

K at Cole, the president of Focus Brands Inc., has one of the most unusual success stories for a business leader. Cole, who leads the multi-billion-dollar parent company of fast food restaurants like Cinnabon and Auntie Anne's Pretzels, started her career as a hostess at Hooters. For readers who may not be familiar with the brand, the American chain is famous for hiring very young and attractive waitresses who serve customers in signature (very short) orange shorts.

Cole, who never graduated college but got an MBA later in her career, achieved her big career break at 19 when she was sent by Hooters to Australia to open its first restaurant there. In the decade she spent at Hooters, Cole told *Forbes* it went from "approximately 100 locations and $300 million in revenue to 500 locations in 33 countries and $1 billion in revenue." She then spent time as president of Cinnabon, another brand that had $1 billion in retail sales, until her promotion at Focus led her to oversee all the group's brands in over 4,000 locations worldwide.

Her meteoric rise from poverty—she was born to a single mother and an alcoholic father—to 36-year-old global business leader is an impressive feat for any gender. No doubt, Cole did a whole lot of "leaning in," to borrow a phrase from Sheryl Sandberg's campaign, to become successful. But Cole says there was another key to her success—working for companies that had strong female leadership at the top.

"In the first 10 years of my business career, every boss I had was female. I had great examples all around me that helped me understand the great variety in the way women leaders show up in the workforce," she tells me. She adds that where companies don't have a visible cadre of female leaders, many women "struggle to come up with their own leadership style." Even junior women, who initially enter a company eyeing a leadership role, lose focus as the subtle message around them is that women rarely succeed at the company—it's hard to be what you don't see, she says.

"Growing up in a company where women were elevated showed me that anything is possible for my career." Cole speaks candidly of her background, where most women in her family "were either truck drivers or in jail, so seeing so many women in suits at work reframed the idea of women's careers," she says.

Another key to Cole's success is being handpicked early for plum assignments and international roles. Going to Australia for Hooters was the first of Cole's international responsibilities and the second time she left her home state. Much of her international success does come down to her own tenacity: "I didn't even have a passport, so I used the 24 hours I had asked for to 'think about the opportunity' to get a passport so I could say yes without them ever knowing I didn't have one." But she says the fact that the company created the opportunity for her to go overseas, "a reason to get a passport, changed my life."

Her early work experiences shaped her leadership qualities today. Cole says she's "courageous to take on new opportunities, culturally sensitive but also doesn't take offense quickly."

It's unusual to see any leader today defy class and educational lines to rise up the ranks in this way. Among female leaders in America, especially, extraordinary educational achievements crop up repeatedly—a degree from Harvard University connects Facebook's Sheryl Sandberg to Google's Susan Wojcicki to former Disney co-chair Anne Sweeney. But pedigree and tenacity alone are still not enough to propel a woman into leadership roles. Even now, among S&P 500 companies, 14.2% of executive officers are women in the U.S., while female CEOs stand at under 5%.

It's not that women aren't receiving the educational pedigree to reach leadership: The number of women entering Harvard Business School (HBS) rose from 25% in 1985 to 41% in 2014. But a study of 25,000 HBS graduates found that of graduates with full-time jobs, men were more likely to hold top jobs with profit and loss responsibility than women.

That is despite the fact that men and women started their careers wanting the same things in terms of job titles, levels of responsibility and professional achievements.

Consider separate data from Catalyst reports on the "glass ceiling" that explores how high-potential women and men MBA graduates fare after business school. With the same prestigious credentials, these women and men should be on equal footing from Day 1 and have similar career trajectories, the report posits. But they don't.

Women MBAs trail their male peers in pay along with advancement opportunities from their very first post-MBA jobs. Overall, they report being less satisfied with their careers. The findings hold even when considering only men and women who did not have children.

Catalyst research also disproves the myth that women aren't "doing the right things to get ahead."

"Does the gender gap persist because women and men adopt different strategies to advance their careers? Are men more proactive? The short answer is no," the report states. When women used the same career advancement strategies as men, they advanced less. Well-known compensation or job growth strategies—such as changing jobs—actually slowed down wage growth for women.

"The only strategy associated with compensation growth for women was ensuring that their manager was aware of their accomplishments—by seeking feedback and credit as appropriate, and asking for a promotion when they felt it was deserved," found the report.

This chapter shows us how the age-old argument that women aren't qualified enough to take on leadership positions is completely outdated. Organizations must rethink leadership by ensuring more women are represented in management roles and given key assignments and roles that are critical to the organization's success. To advance more women into leadership roles, it's not just the woman's responsibility to "lean in"—organizations must "lean in" to the possibility of women as leaders too.

Women In Leadership Roles

Even when women do "all the right things," such as having the best qualifications and asking for promotions, there's another bias that holds them back. It is systemic and yet so subtle that it becomes hard to pinpoint, and therefore, to correct. One of the main barriers to women's advancement, once a woman is able to overcome the hurdles outlined in previous chapters, comes from an unconscious bias that both men and women have: that women don't make good leaders. Because of this, even high-potential women don't get groomed early on for the right roles and assignments that lead to executive positions.

"The 'think leader, think male' mindset is still alive across many organizations," says Deborah Gillis, president and CEO of the nonprofit Catalyst. The view that the command-and-control styles of leadership are most effective, coupled with unconscious biases about how women lead, still present a hurdle in most countries on how to propel more women into executive roles.

In various surveys, female bosses are less liked than male bosses. Americans would prefer a male boss (35%) to a female one (23%), if they were accepting a new job and could choose their boss, found this Gallup study.

Women face a persistent double bind when it comes to their leadership capabilities—she has a higher chance of being liked if she behaves in a "feminine" way, but she's probably not respected or seen as a leader. If she operates in a "masculine" way, however, she's more likely to be called names like "bossy" (or worse) and disliked.

What's alarming is that if a company already has one female executive leader, another woman's chances of landing one of the organization's five highest-paid executive positions falls by 51%, research finds.

"It might very well be the case that male top managers just want to check a box—there is no more effort, no more mentoring, to appoint a second woman to the top management team," Cristian Dezso, an associate professor at the University of Maryland's business school, told *The Wall Street Journal.* "They are one and done."

Dezso's analysis found the percentage of S&P 1500 companies with a female executive leader increased from 1.6% in 1992 to 8.7% in 2011. But among the companies with women in their top five executive jobs, most of them had only one woman in an executive seat.

Just 24 female presidents are in office today among the world's 196 countries. And while 50% of law school attendees today are women, only 20% of the partners at law firms are female.

The Changing Face Of Leadership

There appears to be a growing mismatch between what traits are desired among leaders and the traits exhibited by the people we currently have in leadership positions. While most companies around the world are run by men, most people actually prefer "feminine" leadership styles. That's according to research by John Gerzema and his team of researchers who surveyed 64,000 people in 13 countries on how innovators develop feminine strengths and values to successfully bounce back from economic and social crises. Their findings were captured in the 2012 book *The Athena Doctrine.*

That is not to say that only women make good leaders, or indeed, that all women have these leadership qualities intrinsically. Instead, the studies find that business leaders—male and female—will be most effective in engaging their employees and driving productivity if they possess "feminine" competencies like collaboration, empathy and humility.

The book describes findings that the "ideal modern leader," according to Gerzema's global research, possesses a large number of traits generally considered to be feminine. These traits include selflessness, collaboration, empathy and emotiveness. The least desirable traits in leaders were aggression, independence and pride, which were viewed as masculine. Leaders who were patient, diplomatic and planned for the future were seen as more effective than leaders who displayed political ability.

Other fascinating insights from *The Athena Doctrine* include:

- More companies and individuals value flexibility and openness, due to globalization and technological innovation, which have led to greater transparency.
- A large majority (79%) of people felt that their personal successes were linked to collaborating and sharing credit with others.
- Of the people surveyed, two-thirds believed that "the world would be better if more men thought like women."
- More people distrusted leaders and believe their company's leaders don't care about them.
- Companies must counter growing distrust by championing feminine skills, or what the book calls "Athena qualities" and competencies. These must be incorporated into accepted leadership styles.
- More successful companies will be values-led, with a focus on accountability to society as whole, not just their shareholders.
- Sixty-nine percent of millennials surveyed said they would rather work for a company with a culture and values they admired, even if that meant lesser compensation.

Female Leadership At Alibaba

Gerzema's research surprised me on many levels, because all the countries I've worked in—Singapore, India, the U.K. and the U.S.—have generally favored leaders with a command-and-control leadership style. Now, a growing number of American companies have begun to brand themselves as "inclusive workplaces" where leaders are much more accessible through social media. In contrast, in Asia, a hierarchical leadership structure—where there is little access to those at the top—still prevails at most companies. A 2012 report from the National University of Singapore found that under 21% of women in China held senior-level positions at work.

But recently, Alibaba, a Chinese e-commerce company, has emerged as one of the first few large Asian companies to openly state company values like "customer first" and "teamwork." Alibaba recently catapulted into international attention after completing the largest initial public offering in history. The company's statistics on female employees are impressive:

- Six of 18 Alibaba founders were women, and most have senior management roles.
- Close to 35% of the company's management and 26% of senior management are female.
- Alibaba Group has many top female leaders, including Chief Financial Officer Maggie Wu; Chief Customer Officer Trudy Dai; Chief People Officer Lucy Peng; President of Alibaba.com Wu Mingzhi; and President of China Smart Logistics Judy Tong.
- Women make up 40% of all Alibaba employees.

Having a gender-balanced team wasn't a conscious strategy, but a result of "bringing a collection of the smartest people together" for Alibaba, says Jennifer Kuperman, the company's VP of internal corporate affairs. When 50% of the company's buyers are women and 51% of the sellers on the site are female, having a high representation of female leaders makes business sense.

But aligning the company's image with championing for women has become more of a priority for Alibaba, she says. In May 2015, a few months after its monster IPO, Alibaba hosted a global conference for women in entrepreneurship, bringing speakers from across the globe to Hangzhou, China to convene. Attendees included Arianna Huffington, founder of The Huffington Post Media Group and Phumzile Mlambo-Ngcuka, executive director of U.N. Women.

"The world is a better place because of women's important creations and contributions. We know that women will lead us to a better and brighter future, and we are honored to host so many inspirational women as we work to empower the next generation of female leaders and entrepreneurs in China," Alibaba's chairman Jack Ma was quoted as saying in the conference's press announcement. "Women have been an integral part of Alibaba Group since its inception, and without them, we would not be where we are today."

"Ma likes to say women have intuition and sensitivity, which makes them great leaders," says Kuperman. "He believes you need a mix of human beings to make a company successful and a good mix of male and female leaders to drive innovation." Alibaba practices what it preaches by advancing women into visible leadership roles.

"When our female employees see someone like Lucy Peng [chief people officer], it brings in our line of sight what's possible at the company for other women."

Kuperman also emphasizes Alibaba's "strong culture of moving people around." While not a formal rotational program, she says the company has a history of moving high-potential employees across various business lines that are integral to the business.

Peng, the company's 42-year-old cofounder, was an economics teacher before joining the founding team of Alibaba. She served as chief people officer for the majority of the time since the company was founded, as well as CEO of Ant Financial Services Group. She served as CEO of Alipay, an online payment platform, from January 2010 to February 2013. There's also Judy Tong, senior vice president of Alibaba Group and president of Cainiao Logistics, who joined Alibaba in 2000. Her first job at Alibaba was as a front-desk receptionist. One year later, she started working closely with Peng and held management roles in departments including administrative, operations, human resources and customer service.

Giving Women The Hot Jobs

Alibaba's example presents an important lesson for women's advancement: When women are selected for plum assignments and high-visibility roles with responsibility for key important lines, they have a high likelihood of succeeding within a company.

Catalyst research corroborates this; visible organization-wide projects, mission-critical roles and global assignments are the "hot jobs" that generally lead to advancement for both sexes. Yet the numbers show that women get fewer of these jobs than men.

Catalyst's report, titled "Good Intentions, Imperfect Execution? Women Get Fewer of the Hot Jobs Needed to Advance," found:

- Working on the right projects makes a significant impact on advancement. Men surveyed said they were working on larger and more visible projects that they believed to carry more risk to their companies.

- Men had greater access to mission-critical roles over the course of their careers, including profit and loss responsibility, budget responsibility and management of direct reports.

- Women were given fewer international opportunities. However, when they were offered a global role, they were no more likely than men to turn it down.

While the leadership capabilities of even the most junior male employees are rarely questioned, dangerous assumptions are made about whether a woman would even be interested in taking on these mission-critical or international assignments to advance.

"I met a young woman in India who shared [that] her manager spoke really highly of her work, yet as she looked around she found that her male colleagues were being given high-visibility projects," Catalyst CEO Deborah Gillis tells me. When the woman went to her boss to ask why she wasn't given these opportunities, he reassured her that she was more than qualified for them, but the roles would require her to work outside normal business hours and he feared for her safety. "The woman told me how frustrated she felt about having the choice made for her," Gillis recalls.

India, to be sure, has a different set of obstacles for women to face—safety included—that aren't a consideration in much of the Western world. But even in the U.S., women are systematically lacking access to these business-critical roles, which leads to them being excluded when it's time to fill the top jobs.

This is a problem everywhere; women end up in staff roles that do not lead to the C-suite, according to INSEAD professor of leadership, Herminia Ibarra. Ibarra, who helped research for the World Economic Forum's annual "Corporate Gender Gap Report," said she asked the top human resources person in the biggest companies of 20 OECD countries this question: "Among the assignments that you consider to be business critical/important, what percentage, in your opinion, are currently held by women (e.g., key startups, turnarounds and line roles in key business units or markets)?" The most frequently reported answers were "0-10%" or "not measured," she writes on her blog. While women are not purposefully discriminated against during decision time, the effects of consistently being excluded from business-critical assignments accumulate over time.

To help propel women into leadership roles, companies must "identify mission-critical roles and focus on getting women into those key assignments from the entry level of the pipeline and avoiding channeling mid-career women predominantly into staff roles," Ibarra tells me.

"Many entrenched organizational structures and work practices were designed to fit men's lives and situations at a time when women made up only a very small portion of the workforce," INSEAD's Ibarra writes in a separate *HBR* blog post. "Even career-enhancing international posts often assume a 'trailing spouse' who has no career and can easily move—a family situation much more common for men than for women."

Ibarra advocates for companies to stay away from informal mentoring programs and women's leadership programs that coach women on self-promotion or personal branding. These breed cynicism, she writes in a blog post on her website. Instead, companies can advance women through employing the "70-20-10 rule."

This rule refers to how 70% of a manager's learning and professional development should be honed through on-the-job stretch assignments. Just 20% should come from mentoring and 10% from taking classes.

"Following this rule means focusing on the company's appointment process and succession planning," she writes. Company leaders must know what are the game-changing roles or assignments that are crucial to an executive's development and expose employees to "the company's primary sources of revenue, strategic markets or key products." Here sponsorship becomes key, as the careers of high-potential women are actively managed in a way that they are exposed to these key areas, and therefore have a better shot at being selected for C-suite roles.

Building A Leadership Pipeline At L'Oréal

Innovative companies recognize that having large numbers of female employees does not automatically mean the company advances women. It is not only critical to assess how many women are in leadership positions, but also whether women leaders are represented across departments and business lines. Having women largely concentrated in human resources, but not in engineering, doesn't set a great leadership precedent at a technology company. Instead, sustained efforts must be made to support, expose and advance women in areas that are critical to the business' bottom line.

I spoke with L'Oréal Paris USA about how it was able to propel women into leadership roles across business lines. A vast majority, 65% of L'Oréal USA employees, are women—nearly half of its global brands are managed by women, and 70% of its global research and innovation workforce is comprised of women. L'Oréal's global board of directors is also 40% women, compared to the industry average of 17%.

It would make sense that many women would work at a beauty company whose products are bought largely by women. But more than just selling products, L'Oréal's mission to be technology-driven has been central to its success. Having employees with concentrations in science, technology, engineering and mathematics (STEM)—areas that women are traditionally underrepresented in—is of core importance to its business.

Recognizing that advancing women in these fields would present a challenge, L'Oréal USA put a number of programs in place to develop high-potential women in STEM. Angela Guy, SVP of diversity and inclusion at L'Oréal USA, tells me about two.

Since 1998, the company's For Women in Science program has recognized and rewarded more than 2,000 female post-doctoral scientists in over 100 countries for their contributions in STEM fields, Guy says. "For the last decade, the company's flagship brand, L'Oréal Paris, has celebrated extraordinary women in the U.S. for their innovative approaches to tackling significant issues and hardships in their local communities."

To encourage entrepreneurship and women in technology, the company also created the Women in Digital program, which, according to the L'Oréal USA website, "promotes, supports and recruits female entrepreneurs by providing them with the opportunity to launch and scale new technologies and digital innovations in partnership with L'Oréal to impact the future of the tech and beauty industries."

Internally, Guy tells me, ensuring women are developed at every level of the pipeline towards leadership is of key importance to the company.

"We track talent regularly and develop customized training programs based on areas of expertise," she says. The company strategizes on formal succession planning and encourages internal mobility—both vertically and laterally, to promote cross-function mobility that helps prepare the company's leadership pipeline for larger roles. "For instance, we're taking marketers and shifting them into digital roles; we're exposing communications professionals to finance, and leveraging other disciplines to ensure our leaders have the broadest backgrounds."

Guy also points to the strides made in the company's operations, traditionally a male-dominated field. L'Oréal USA now has nearly equal representation in supply chain and operations overall—from plant managers and purchasing agents to financial managers and project engineers.

"L'Oréal USA's first female plant manager is also one of the founding members of Women in Leadership— Operations, an internal organization dedicated to empowering, retaining and developing future female leaders in operations through a series of yearly interactive events. It's a networking opportunity for L'Oréal women to hear inspirational presentations, participate in discussions and to learn the qualities of successful leaders," she says.

Rethinking What Leadership Looks Like

This chapter has created links between pre-existing assumptions about what makes a good leader and why high-potential women are often denied the very opportunities they need to be successful. As Ibarra writes in her blog post, "How work is valued may similarly give men an advantage: Research indicates that organizations tend to ignore or undervalue behind-the-scenes work (building a team, avoiding a crisis), which women are more likely to do, while rewarding heroic work, which is most often done by men."

While the practices were not intended to discriminate, the cumulative effect comes at a grave disadvantage to women who would otherwise make top leaders. "A vicious cycle ensues: Men appear to be best suited to leadership roles, and this perception propels more of them to seek and attain such positions, thus reinforcing the notion that they are simply better leaders," Ibarra writes.

Instead, organizations must take a good look at which leadership styles are represented at the company today. Chances are, male leaders still prevail and a more aggressive, masculine style of leadership is rewarded. It's crucial for companies to assess whether this leadership style will continue to drive success, especially as we're moving towards a society where transparency and collaboration continue to be valued.

As more women are represented in the company's upper echelons, junior female employees see proof that a multitude of leadership styles are celebrated.

This is also an important way to eliminate the "Queen Bee syndrome," a phenomenon in which female executives in male-dominated environments are unwilling to help others succeed. A staggering 95% of the 1,000 women surveyed by the American Management Association in 2011 said they had felt undermined by other women at some point in their careers. This is often due to a corporate culture where there are very few women at the top, so those who do make it to senior leadership are often unwilling to help—or worse, sabotage—other women.

But in organizations with a collaborative leadership style and more than just a token few women in management, this message is reversed. "Women who have had the support and mentorship of other women help other women," Catalyst's Gillis tells me.

Today's senior leaders must also make an unwavering commitment to ensure that deserving women are given all the right tools—the business-critical "hot jobs"—to advance them towards leadership roles.

Focus Brands' Kat Cole, who benefited from "hot jobs" and international assignments, has in turn spent a significant proportion of her leadership capital in developing other female leaders at her organization. Within a year of her tenure as Cinnabon CEO, Cole's team was 80% female, until she had to "purposefully start hiring more men to balance it out," she says.

Now from her executive position, she says she is particularly thoughtful about building a company culture that values feminine leadership styles as much as masculine traits.

"Because I'm diverse, I put a lot of responsibility on how I show up every day," she tells me. "I like to show other women that getting ahead here is also about being kind and accessible. If they see a woman at the top whose leadership style is approachable, that really helps build an inclusive company culture where they can aspire to top positions too."

8

WOMEN IN THE C-SUITE AND BOARD

Women around the world are now the heads of more governments and corporations than at any point in recorded history. Yet, when I searched for "CEO" on Shutterstock, one of the world's largest online repositories for stock photos, the overwhelming majority of images were of white men. On the first page of my search, no women of color even featured on the list. Our association with the word "chief executive" is inherently male. Excerpts from a recent conversation I had while researching for this book highlight our entrenched ideas on what a leader should look like:

"I'm interviewing a CEO today," I told a friend as I walked out of the house.
He responded: "Great, what time are you meeting him?"
"Her," I corrected.

My friend wasn't wrong in making this mistake. The knee-jerk reaction to the word continues to be white and male—fewer large companies in America are run by women than by men named John. For every female executive in an S&P 1500 firm, you will find four men named John, Robert, William or James.

Across 3,000 global companies assessed by Credit Suisse, just 3.9% of CEOs are female. Women heading major business departments globally stand at 8.5%, and women hold a mere 17.5% of top strategic and financial roles. Meanwhile, women lead 18.9% of "shared services" jobs—ones that don't have a direct route to the C-suite, such as legal, human resources and marketing units.

However, more women than ever before are armed with the qualifications, experience and, most of all, desire to lead companies. So why the lack of female representation at the top?

Compounded with much of the research I highlighted in earlier chapters, women face several obstacles in advancing to the highest levels of the company. But even when women are just a few levels shy of the C-suite, they often lack the critical support and sponsorship to get to the executive office, Julie Nugent, Catalyst VP and leader of the Catalyst Research Center, tells me. "Our research also shows unconscious biases baked into things like performance assessments that disadvantage women and employees of color," she adds—the same type of unconscious bias that automatically causes most people to equate the word "CEO" with "male."

The CEO I was interviewing that day happened to be a woman: Liz Pearce, the 38-year-old leader of software company LiquidPlanner. Pearce represents the changing face of what it is to be CEO: "I'm younger than everyone on my management team," she tells me.

With stints at PlayStation, Google and Amazon, Pearce credits much of her rise to leadership to working for "very strong women." Seeing is believing, according to Pearce, and constantly seeing successful women rising up the ranks at all the companies she had worked for challenged her to push her career to new heights.

Ultimately it wasn't the lack of leadership opportunities, but long (and increasingly longer) working hours that made Pearce rethink her initial goal of rising to executive positions within these corporations. "With the desire of creating a life to be personally and professionally fulfilled," even before she had children, Pearce set up her own marketing consultancy for technology companies.

That's when the founders of LiquidPlanner, a small Seattle startup, approached her. The two male founders, Charles Seybold and Jason Carlson, recognized Pearce's talents early. They championed relentlessly for her, first bringing her in as a consultant who created the company's first go-to-market strategy, then—you guessed it— sponsored her through the organization to become vice president of sales and marketing and then chief operating officer. Ultimately, Seybold stepped down as CEO and nominated Pearce to take over the company's reins in 2012, after she had been there for six years.

"I didn't start at LiquidPlanner to be CEO ... but I found something that I loved to do and that was building businesses," she says.

When I interviewed Pearce in her Seattle office, overlooking a stunning view of Lake Washington, I felt like I was speaking to a friend, not a CEO of a multi-million-dollar company. Many male technology leaders I've met on the West Coast wear jeans and exude an aura of casualness. Women leading these companies are still scarce and walk a narrow tightrope between being considered "one of the geeks" and feminine enough. Pearce mentions this in the interview, emphasizing how the company culture makes a big difference in how far and fast women advance. As a leader, she's easygoing and forthright, but she's clearly a force to be reckoned with. The company's tools are used by over 2,000 organizations around the world and posted double-digit revenue growth last year.

Pearce tackles the leadership obstacles that come with being a young woman in an executive position with humor—she's regularly mistaken for a more junior staff member. She's also gotten comfortable with often being the only woman in the room during meetings with other CEOs. "But there's definitely confusion if I'm standing with an older white guy who looks more like their idea of a CEO."

Instead, she sees the positives—being female has been intrinsic to her goal of building a culture of inclusive leadership. According to her, the senior leadership team has the most responsibility in creating a culture that encourages and rewards ambitious women.

"There's a lot of subtle ways you can encourage women to rise. I love to be challenged by women [I work with]. If someone will go up against me on something they really believe in … that's who I want in charge," she says. While many corporate cultures still operate so that women are dissuaded to speak up, or even penalized for it, it ultimately rests on the shoulders of a company's leaders to show that different points of views are welcomed there. There are ways to accept and reward women's leadership styles—simply by acknowledging and showing approval when you are challenged in meetings, she says. "You can create a culture where people express their opinions and points of view openly and constructively."

Female employees accounted for 67% of the promotions at LiquidPlanner in the last year. "Employment is a two-way street. You're doing something for them, but they should be doing something for you, which is the chance to expand your mind, your experience, your perspective on the world."

Pearce leads with confidence and easily laughs off the times she's mistaken for a junior employee. But she still stands out as an outlier as one of the very few woman leaders of a fast-growing B2B software company. Even among technology firms with a modern corporate culture, few women—if at all—are able to progress to the C-suite or board.

The fact is that the glass ceiling still remains intact for most women in executive positions around the world. As a result, many high-potential women stop aiming for the C-suite altogether.

Cultural Barriers To The C-suite

In a global survey of 1,421 executives, McKinsey research concluded that companies fail their diversity objectives due to cultural obstacles. According to the survey, female executives aim as high as men when it comes to their career aspirations: Of all mid- or senior-level women, 79% (and 81% of men) expressed a desire to reach top management. "Senior women executives just one step away from the C-suite are more likely to agree strongly that they have top-management ambitions," the report states.

But the survey also showed that many were less confident they would make it there: While 86% of men were certain they could reach the C-suite, only 69% of women were.

What makes the difference? The leadership style of their company. Women who were self-assured they would succeed said that management at their companies was more accommodating to women's leadership and communication styles, and both genders were equally likely to reach the top.

In contrast, lack of diversity in terms of leadership styles was an obstacle for many women, according to the report:

"Almost 40% of female respondents said that women's leadership and communication styles don't fit with the prevailing model of top management in their companies.

Performance models for work-life balance issues also tilt against women. Most men and women agree that a top-level career implies 'anytime, anywhere' availability to work and that this imposes a particularly severe penalty on female managers. When asked whether having children is compatible with a top-level career for women, 62% of all respondents agree—but a much larger share (80%) think that's true for men."

The business case for having greater female representation in the executive ranks has never been stronger. There's direct correlation between diversity and a company's financial performance.

In the previously-cited Credit Suisse research, summarized by the *Washington Post* here, the firm tracked 28,000 executives in 40 countries and correlated their findings to financial performance.

The research found a link between companies with more female executives and higher returns on equity (ROE), market valuations, higher stock performance and dividend payouts.

In comparing data from companies where women hold under 5% of the top operational jobs to those where key roles are held by more than 10% of women, it found a 27%

higher ROE and a 42% higher ratio of dividend payouts for those with more diverse gender representation.

Why Diversity Of Thought Matters

Financial performance alone may not be the only way to assess the positive impact of a diverse team. A new body of research shows the next frontier of innovation is about diversity of thought and it is essential for a company to retain its competitive advantage.

Diversity of thought, a term coined by Deloitte Consulting, states that by combining different thinkers—analytical with creative, "big-picture" folks with the detail-oriented ones—companies can stimulate creativity and drive efficiency. The belief that our thinking, and ability to innovate, is shaped by our culture, background, experiences and personalities is the core tenet of diversity of thought.

"Diversity of thought goes beyond the affirmation of equality—simply recognizing differences and responding to them. Instead, the focus is on realizing the full potential of people, and in turn, the organization, by acknowledging and appreciating the potential promise of each person's unique perspective and different way of thinking," finds the study.

As a result, leaders and organizations must be prepared to accept that there's not just "one right way" to get things done. Companies need to focus on leveraging the myriad differences among their employees to be truly innovative and inclusive, states the Deloitte research.

A different study had similar conclusions. A study by the Center for Talent Innovation looked at two types of diversity: inherent and acquired. "Inherent diversity involves traits you are born with, such as gender, ethnicity and sexual orientation," states a *Harvard Business Review* article summarizing the study. "Acquired diversity involves traits you gain from experience: Working in another country can help you appreciate cultural differences, for example, while selling to female consumers can give you gender smarts."

Companies with "two-dimensional diversity," in which leaders have at least three inherent and three acquired diversity traits, innovate and perform better than others. "Employees at these companies are 45% likelier to report that their firm's market share grew over the previous year and 70% likelier to report that the firm captured a new market," the article says.

"2-D diversity unlocks innovation by creating an environment where 'outside the box' ideas are heard," wrote the Center's CEO Sylvia Ann Hewlett, in the *Harvard Business Review* blog post. "When minorities form a critical mass and leaders value differences, all employees can find senior people to go to bat for compelling ideas and can persuade those in charge of budgets to deploy resources to develop those ideas."

Diverse Leadership At Coca-Cola Enterprises

Diverse and inclusive leadership teams have been a characteristic of all the teams John Brock, the CEO and chairman of Coca-Cola Enterprises (CCE), built throughout his career. The head of the $10 billion beverage bottling company formerly held executive roles at Procter & Gamble, Cadbury Schweppes and InBev.

I first heard Brock speak about his experience and commitment to diversity in corporate America in 2012, at TEDxWomen Atlanta. I was blown away to see a white man in his 60s, born in the American south, get up on stage to passionately make the case for how developing and advancing women leaders is good for business. As a young, female banking and finance reporter that year in Atlanta, often when I brought up women's leadership during CEO interviews, the topic would quickly be brushed off.

Brock was one of the first male leaders of a Top 500 company to actively and relentlessly discuss female leadership. During the interview for this book, he repeatedly mentioned his belief that engaging leaders who have diversity of thought is a key contributor to the company's success. CCE's market capitalization is over $10 billion.

"Diversity and inclusion in organizations is a real driver of better decision-making," he tells me. One-third of CCE's leadership team and board of directors are female.

Brock shares three recommendations on building a diverse team:

1. Always consider a diverse slate of candidates. Admittedly it isn't always easy to find qualified diverse candidates, but that's never a good excuse for not having a diverse leadership team, he tells me. Brock would know— he has always needed to hire leaders with a sound understanding of technology, infrastructure and engineering. He suggests that *all* leaders should state their intention to hire or promote from a diverse pool.

"We have four women on a board and I was completely invested in strategies to find those women. I said to our search firms in no uncertain terms that I wanted to see a diverse slate of candidates," he says. Just stating that intention can make all the difference—especially when hiring for the very top levels of any organization, which is always done in collaboration with partners.

2. Commit to diversity from the top.

"We have established targets in our latest sustainability report that 40% of our leadership and management positions in 2025 must be filled by women," he says. "By the way, that's all because we'll drive business performance by doing that." By setting a target, the company is able to evaluate, year on year, the number of women who need to be advanced each year to make the goal.

Getting more women into leadership is a company-wide effort that starts from the highest levels of the organization, he tells me. "Once you hire women in, you have to have focused strategies on keeping them. Often businesses will hire really terrific women and they will leave. Developing flexible work, work-sharing—for both men and women—it's absolutely critical to our success."

Brock tells me one of his earliest commitments was to establish women's networks in all of CCE's locations around the world, where he regularly visits and addresses the group. Brock also encourages male and female board members to address the CCE's women's groups. Leading women are identified and elevated through the company's robust women's networks.

"It's about developing a complete program across the organization to advocate for women," he emphasizes.

3. Tie diversity back to business.

Brock doesn't mince his words when he talks about the positive impact of having a diverse leadership team.

"If you look at our business results over the last five years, we've measurably outperformed the S&P and Dow from a share price standpoint and having women in significant leadership positions was critically important to that," he says.

Business Drives Diversity At Kimberly-Clark

In 2009, Kimberly-Clark Corp., the company that owns Huggies diapers, Kleenex tissues and Kotex sanitary napkins, had a surprising revelation. After analyzing data, it found that just 17% of its director-level and above employees were women—a cause for concern, as 85% of its target consumers are female.

A year later, Sue Dodsworth was promoted to global chief diversity officer, with a mandate to foster greater diversity to drive business results. According to her, the best results come from when diversity is championed throughout the organization. Dodsworth adds that building diverse teams was constantly emphasized as a business priority by Tom Falk, the CEO.

To do that, more high-potential women were advanced to decision-making leadership teams. "We made a conscious effort to recruit and retain more women and ensure more women were taking on the hot jobs, responsible for profit and loss and functional roles," she says. Dodsworth herself, an employee for over 13 years, has worked across three continents and held "seven significantly different roles in different functions that helped me develop a broad perspective and understanding of different parts of the business."

The company seems to have made big strides in this realm. Within four years, it reports that women make up 30% of director-and-above employees. Five out of nine members of the senior leadership team at the company are women, including its CFO and chief supply chain officer. Kimberly-

Clark also won the 2014 Catalyst Inc. award for advancing women.

"Diversity is not a project or initiative here, it is in our culture and is pushiest from our board and C-suite. Our success to date is because we made it a business strategy, not a HR strategy," she says, pointing to the company's share price, which has close to doubled in the last five years.

Women On Boards

The topic of women and boards, whether to have set quotas or not, has sparked an international conversation around board diversity. Some countries favor legislative mandates, quotas for the number of female directors. While many Scandinavian companies adopted this model, in a surprising move, India's financial regulatory body imposed a quota of at least one female director on the board of every listed firm, with a strict deadline to comply or be fined, in 2014.

Having more women on company boards—whether a 100,000-person public company headquartered in the U.S. or a private company of 100 employees based in Singapore, remains a major challenge and opportunity.

First, the statistics. The number of women on corporate boards around the world coincides with the small number of women in leadership positions. Western Europe leads, according to Catalyst data, with Norwegian women holding 35.5% of board seats. Finland has 29.9% and France is third, with 29.7%. But in Japan, only 3.1% of board seats are occupied by women. This is an alarming statistic, given the high education and literacy rate in the country, but perhaps less surprising when considering traditional gender roles in Japanese society. Women hold 19% of seats among the S&P 500 companies in America. This is truly troubling as this index represents some of the most profitable and global companies in the world, but many do not have a single female board member.

Women serving on corporate boards can drive business performance. A 2012 Credit Suisse report reveals fascinating insights on the correlation between stock prices and women on boards. According to the *Huffington Post* article summarizing the study, "The stock prices of small and mid-size companies with at least one female board member have performed 17% better over the past six years than those without one. ... The difference is even wider at large companies, where female-friendly boards perform 26% better." While year-on-year data has shown improvement in female representation on corporate boards, there's much work to be done.

Some of the fastest-growing and most innovative companies are lagging more traditional industries in board diversity. In Silicon Valley, 43% of the top 150 companies by revenue do not have a single female director on board. Some entrepreneurs are taking matters into their own hands to change the ratio. Serial entrepreneur Sukhinder Singh Cassidy launched Boardlist, a database of 700 qualified female board candidates. Facebook COO Sheryl Sandberg and venture capitalist Marc Andreessen came up with a boot camp, in partnership with Stanford University, to equip women and minorities with the skills to sit on other company and startup boards. Initiatives like these can be valuable, but are still part of the "fix women" mentality, or could result in so-called "golden skirts," where the same women are repeatedly approached to take on multiple directorships, without pipeline development for less experienced women who could be future directors.

Instead, there are several measures that companies can also take to ensure board diversity, says Deb DeHaas, chief inclusion officer and national managing partner for the Center for Corporate Governance at Deloitte LLP.

Recommendations from DeHaas, who has served two terms on Deloitte's U.S. board and several large nonprofit boards:

1. Focus on skills, not titles.

"The view that board roles can only be served by a CEO or CFO means that only a relatively small number of women in public companies can serve," says DeHaas. Instead, boards should focus on choosing members with a variety of relevant skills and not only choose from a narrow pool based on the candidate's job title.

2. Position women as candidates.

Deloitte research finds that 72% of new board members are selected after being recommended by existing board members. Having the current CEO and board members advocating for female candidates could be a critical step in changing the numbers.

"One of the best ways to position women for board roles is through the sponsorship of the current CEO and chairman of the board," she says. "I've seen successful situations when a CEO has shortlist of individuals that includes women and other diverse candidates. The support of the CEO in positioning diverse candidates for these roles is key."

3. Draw from a diverse pool.

When searching for board candidates, it's necessary to "look broadly and outside your typical networks." DeHaas says a number of organizations maintain a pool of board-ready female candidates, such as Women Corporate Directors, a global organization of women corporate board directors.

4. Prepare women to become board-ready.
DeHaas says forward-thinking organizations will help high-potential women develop the necessary skills to become board-ready by exposing them to business-critical assignments. "Looking to help develop and leverage some of those sought-after skills is a great way to add women to that shortlist when selecting board members," she says. These include ensuring women spend time developing:

- Operating experience
- Profit and loss experience
- Financial experience
- Deep industry experience

"It's important to consider the development plans for senior executives as a board development opportunity," she adds.

LiquidPlanner's Pearce has one more suggestion: Select high-potential women in your organization to become board observers. When Pearce was VP of marketing and sales, the company's former CEO would invite her to attend company board meetings so she could be exposed to the inner workings of the boardroom. When it came time for her own appointment, she was already a recognizable face among existing board members.

Quota Or Not?

Experts in this arena often spar on the efficacy of board quotas. Does a legal requirement for companies to have more female directors help create more equality in the boardroom?

Not necessarily, according to one camp. Norway passed a law in 2006, mandating women to hold 40% of public boardroom seats. However, 40% of businesses converted into private companies to avoid the quota. When asked about this change, two-thirds of these companies admitted the quota rules had influenced their decision to delist from the stock exchange. Still, the fact that Norway leads the pack globally in number of women directors must mean they're doing something right.

India's director quota was initially applauded as a step forward for women's rights in South Asia. Unfortunately, there were reports that many large companies mishandled the situation when company leaders elected their mothers, sisters and wives as a last resort to fulfill the requirements.

Still, having more women, even those not necessarily elected fairly, could give India's companies a boost in getting more women into leadership roles—a boost that is sorely needed, as India consistently features as one of the countries with the lowest female participation in the workforce.

"I'm watching closely how the law will influence policies and what will the impact of the diverse board be on how companies in India engage with women," Shachi Irde, executive director of Catalyst India, tells me. "I think some dynamic changes from having more women on board would be greater promotion of more women to senior levels. It's inspirational and aspirational to have more women succeed."

A study by BNY Mellon found that quotas may boost the number of women on boards but don't ensure that they will stay. Instead, the study finds that the most effective way